EUGENIE
CLARK

Marine Biologist

Ronald A. Reis

Ferguson
An imprint of ☑ˈFacts On File

Eugenie Clark: Marine Biologist

Ferguson
An imprint of Facts On File, Inc.
132 West 31st Street
New York NY 10001

Library of Congress Cataloging-in-Publication Data
Reis, Ronald A.
   Eugenie Clark: marine biologist / Ronald A. Reis.
      p. cm.
  Includes bibliographical references and index.
   ISBN 0–8160–5883–0 (hc : alk. paper)
  1. Clark, Eugenie—Juvenile literature. 2. Ichthyologists—United States—
Biography—Juvenile literature. 3. Marine biologists—United States—Biography—
Juvenile literature. I. Title
QL31 C56R45 2005
578.77'092—dc22

                                                2004016076

Ferguson books are available at special discounts when purchased in bulk quantities for businesses, associations, institutions, or sales promotions. Please call our Special Sales Department in New York at (212) 967-8800 or (800) 322-8755.

You can find Ferguson on the World Wide Web at http://www.fergpubco.com

Text design by David Strelecky

Pages 81–113 adapted from Ferguson's *Encyclopedia of Careers and Vocational Guidance, Twelfth Edition.*

Printed in the United States of America

MP TB 10 9 8 7 6 5 4 3 2 1

This book is printed on acid-free paper.

CONTENTS

1

TO CATCH A SHARK

The shark line extends the length of a football field, two miles offshore Florida in the Gulf of Mexico. Sixteen loops have been evenly spaced, with a quick-release becket knot, side line, and hook attached. Dangling from each 2 $^1/_4$ inch steel claw hangs the bait, a juicy gray mullet, which is a delicious shark appetizer.

Eugenie "Genie" Clark and Beryl Chadwick begin to examine each hook in turn, as the two bob in their 21-foot Chris-Craft boat, the *Dancer*. The first hook is empty. So are the second, the third, and the fourth.

"After a few more hooks, I saw Beryl straining to pull up the next side line," recalls Genie, in her book *The Lady and the Sharks*. "Beryl grabbed the line. The line jumped. Several feet below, a large white object was coming up through the water. The line led into the mouth on the underside of a shark. It was still alive, and as the jaws moved, we could plainly see triangular serrated teeth. The shark was about 11 feet long and looked to weigh 500 pounds. From that moment on, I knew I was in the shark-hunting business."

On that day, late in January 1955, 32-year-old marine biologist Dr. Eugenie Clark, founder and director of the Cape Haze Marine Laboratory in Placida, Florida, had indeed discovered a new passion. Earlier, she had received a phone call from Dr. John H. Heller, a medical doctor doing cancer research on shark livers. "He was in the Caribbean, in 'shark-infested waters,' looking for shark livers for his research," Genie remembers. "He wanted to know if I knew how to catch a shark, and if so, would I help him capture one or two?"

Though already an accomplished ichthyologist (a scientist who studies fish), with a Ph.D in zoology and extensive diving experience in the South Pacific and Red Sea, up until now Genie's involvement with sharks was limited. That, however, would all change. In the coming years, this woman working in a male-dominated profession would gain international fame as the Shark Lady, that is, one of the world's premier authorities on shark behavior.

A Shark's World

Although the lion is king of the jungle, in the world's oceans the shark is at the top of the food chain. The shark knows no predator—except humans. Feared and misunderstood for

Dr. Eugenie Clark, the "Shark Lady," is a premier expert on shark behavior. (University Publications, University of Maryland)

centuries, this fierce hunter of the watery world has been around, in its present form, for more than 200 million years.

Sharks come in all sizes. One, like the luminously spined pygmy shark, is only 4 inches long and can easily fit into your palm. The whale shark, on the other hand, is the largest fish in the world. Measuring up to 59 feet and weighing 13 tons (though the average is 25 feet long and 9 tons), this harmless gentle giant of flesh and cartilage is as long as a large school bus.

There are about 400 shark species. Small or large, sharks are indeed amazing creatures. In addition to having the same five senses as humans (sight, hearing, smell, taste, and touch), sharks have inherited two additional senses that we do not possess. They can detect minute electric signals emanating from all living creatures. Some sharks can respond to a signal as low as a hundred-millionth of a volt per centimeter—a minuscule amount. In addition, sharks have an acute sense of vibration. Sharks can easily pick up distant disturbances in water that are made by struggling fish or the erratic movements of human swimmers. These two senses make sharks especially good hunters.

Sharks are carnivores, meaning they only eat meat; that meat can be anything from the smallest zooplankton to the largest whales to human beings. There are only about 100 reported shark attacks on humans each year, about 10

Sharks know no predators—except humans. Pictured above is a grey nurse shark. (Landov)

of which result in death. When a biting does occur, it is mostly on the arms, hands, legs, and feet—not surprising, since 31 percent of shark attacks take place in waist-deep water. The victim often tries to fend off the shark with his or her hands or by kicking. Though rare, there are times when people have been swallowed whole.

A Lifelong Career

It was into this shark world that Genie ventured, studying sharks' habits and dispelling the many misconceptions that surround them. For well over a half-century, this remarkable woman has gone out among the ocean's inhabitants, armed, in some cases, with only a pair of goggles and a spear. Though she is an accomplished swimmer, who once said she considered herself a diver first and a scientist second, Genie has received remarkable recognition as both a descriptive writer of exceptional clarity and as a highly respected scientist. She has led a fulfilling and exciting life and has broken down many occupational barriers for women. She is a woman who took a childhood interest in the animal world (bringing home a dead rat and monkey for dissection) and propelled it into a lifelong career. Her story is one of adventure and discovery.

2

AQUARIUM ADVENTURES

The gray brick Battery Park Aquarium in lower Manhattan looked like a medieval castle. The year was 1931, and then-nine-year-old Genie Clark entered this temple of the aquatic for the first time on an eventful Saturday morning.

Genie's mother took her to the aquarium for amusement. The young girl was soon immersed in a misty watery wonderland, which she had hardly known existed. "All about me were glass tanks with moving creatures in them," she recalls. "At the back was a tank larger than the others, and the water in it was less clear, more mysterious. It was pale green and, a few feet from the glass wall that I looked through, it went on and on. Leaning over the brass railing, I brought my face as close as possible to the glass and pretended I was walking on the bottom of the sea."

The aquarium's tanks were filled with all types of marine life, from streamlined, fast-swimming fish, to sluggish, bottom-creeping forms. And there was a shark. It was the first live shark Genie had ever seen, but it would certainly not be her last.

Swimming Like a Fish

Eugenie Clark was born on May 4, 1922, in New York City. Her mother, Yumiko, was Japanese, and her father, Charles Clark, was American. Genie's parents had met at a private swimming pool, where Yumiko was working as a swimming instructor. Charles was the manager who hired her.

Two years after Genie's birth, tragedy struck the family when Charles died. Genie, her mother, and her grandmother, Yuriko, were forced to move into a tiny apartment. Yumiko had to go to work and become the family's breadwinner.

Although times were tough for the Clark family, Genie was not neglected. Her mother helped her explore many activities. Yumiko was an excellent swimmer, and she wanted Genie to follow in her footsteps. By the age of two, Genie was swimming in the ocean. Genie's early saltwater frolicking was a sign of things to come.

During their ocean swims together, Genie's mother introduced her to the "gum plug" technique for keeping water out of her ears. "Chewing gum can be molded to the exact shape of the ear opening, as a plug to keep the water out," Genie remembers. "The natural wax prevents it from sticking to the ear. I got a big kick out of the ritual of sitting on the beach with mama while we chewed gum and then plugged it into our ears before our first dip. It made me feel like a professional swimmer."

In elementary school, Genie excelled academically. She even skipped a grade. But when it came to being cooperative, Genie wasn't quite as successful. Genie entertained her fellow students with tales of her atypical eating habits that stemmed from her Japanese heritage. She would shock them by describing her seaweed breakfasts and ground-shark-cake dinners. Her school lunch bag often included sashimi (raw fish). At times Genie was teased about her lunches, and nasty remarks were made about her Japanese ancestry, but the feisty girl sometimes fought back, even physically. Although she received almost all A's in her classes, she received the occasional F in conduct and made more than one visit to the principal's office.

Yumiko was now working at a newsstand in downtown Manhattan, and Genie was often required to accompany her mother on Saturday mornings. Genie tried to keep herself entertained, but she soon became bored. Not wanting her daughter to loiter alone on the waterfront, Yumiko hit upon the simple idea of sending her daughter to the nearby aquarium to while away the mornings until lunchtime. This was to begin a period of personal discovery for Genie, leading to a lifelong fascination with all creatures, great and small, in the deep.

An Aquarium of Her Own

The 1930s was the decade of the Great Depression. At the height of this tough economic period, one in four adult Americans was unemployed. At the Battery Park Aquarium Genie met a number of these down-and-out individuals. She often acted as their tutor, explaining aquarium exhibits to the homeless people who sought shelter in the aquarium from the bitter winter cold. Genie's skills as a future teacher began to surface.

Despite these challenging times, the Clarks still exchanged Christmas gifts every year. And as always, Genie prepped her mother to provide the "perfect" gift.

"I coaxed her into buying me a large 15-gallon aquarium," Genie recollects in *Lady with a Spear*. "We had to get some gravel and a few large stones to give the bottom a 'natural' look, a variety of aquatic plants including the emerald long-leaved Vallisneria, and some coral-red snails. It was the most exciting spending spree either of us had ever known."

Things didn't stop there. "We picked out a pair of veil-tailed guppies, black-speckled red platies, pale green swordtails, striped danios, iridescent pearl danios, 'head-and-tail lights,' a weird looking scavenger fish with

The Battery Park Aquarium in New York, 1930 (Corbis)

'whiskers,' and a pair of graceful angelfish," Genie continues. "When I saw a clown fish I wanted, my mother informed me that we were way over what she had planned to spend for Christmas. Nonetheless, I got her to agree to let it count for my birthday present as well."

Fish-Breeding Business

As the months and years progressed, Genie and her mother became even more interested in aquariums and fish. Collecting fascinating aquatic creatures and watching them breed and grow was turning into quite a hobby.

However, it seems an aquarium alone was not enough for Genie. Soon, she and a friend from high school had created their own *terrarium,* an enclosure similar to an aquarium, but which is a home for land animals.

The salamanders were the first to arrive. Some of these tailed amphibians can live up to 50 years. Others, like the ones Genie had, were fast growing. Then there was the horned toad, which lived in a glass cage the two called the "desert."

And, of course, they had an alligator. Genie describes the lizard like this: "Our alligator gave his aquarium the atmosphere of a jungle river. I would stare at him as he lay in the water, with only his eyes and snout above the surface, and he would seem to grow until he became a large, ferocious reptile. But then he would open his jaws wide and in place of the mighty roar of a giant alligator came a squeaky 'oink'—and he shrank back again to baby size."

While Genie was in high school (where her favorite subject was biology) she was completely immersed in everything aquatic. She became the youngest member ever accepted into the Queens County Aquarium Society. She began to keep meticulous records of all her pets, their scientific names, the date she got each specimen, and what happened to it. Her hobby was becoming serious, indeed.

Around this time Genie acquired a pair of Siamese fighting fish, the "winged" air-breathing fish that come to the surface for air. Before long, the male had built a bubble nest at the surface of the water. Carefully, he then wrapped his mate with his long flowing fins, squeezing her body until the eggs dropped out. A few days later, Genie and her mother watched as microscopic baby fish appeared. There were hundreds of them. "I thought of selling my family on the idea of going into the fish-breeding business," Genie declared, only half seriously. Nothing, however, was to come of that venture.

Expanding Ambitions

As Genie advanced through high school, her interests and career goals became more focused and determined. In her biology classes, Genie was learning the fundamentals about plants and animals that would give her a greater understanding of the many creatures taking up room in the family's small apartment. As she remembers it, referring to the Siamese fighting fish, "I could now visualize what took place in that bubble nest from the time the male fish blew the eggs into the bubbles until the time [when] two hundred dollars' worth of tiny tails appeared."

Genie also did well in English. "No matter what topic we were told to write about for our class compositions, I could usually slant the subject to bring in fish," she recalls. Later in her career, Genie would write hundreds of scientific papers, numerous popular articles for magazines such as *National Geographic,* and three books.

Although her courses were important to her training, an inspiring mentor, who pointed the way by example, was equally important. Genie found inspiration in the writings of William Beebe, considered by many to be a born naturalist (a scientist who studies natural history, especially zoology and botany). He became Genie's hero in her high-school years.

Beebe was born in 1877 in Brooklyn, New York. Just as Genie's eyes were opened to the natural world by her early visits to the Battery Park Aquarium, Beebe gained similar experiences at the American Museum of Natural History. His primary early interests were in *ornithology,* the study of birds, and in *taxidermy,* the preparation, stuffing, and mounting of animals.

In his early twenties, Beebe began helmet diving. He soon became obsessed with the desire to dive ever deeper, where he would see strange marine animals in their natural deep-sea habitat. Beebe partnered with an engineer, Otis Barton, who also wanted to explore the ocean depths. Together, they designed a device called the bathysphere, which means "deep sphere." Essentially a hollow, airtight steel "ball," a mere four feet, nine inches in diameter, with walls one-and-a-half-feet thick, the bathysphere barely had room to hold two divers. The two-porthole, 5,000-pound casing was pressurized. Once you were sealed inside, you could descend to incredible depths and do so while wearing ordinary clothes. Tethered to a single 3,500-foot cable, the bathysphere was dropped overboard, to reach down as far as possible. On August 15, 1934, William Beebe and Otis Barton made themselves world-famous by descending 3,028 feet beneath the ocean surface, deep

Dr. William Beebe (left) and John T. Vann with the bathysphere. Beebe inspired Genie to one day explore the deep sea. (Associated Press)

into the blackness of the twilight (mesopelagic) zone, the home of lantern fish, hatchet fish, squid, and octopus.

Beebe went on to write numerous popular articles and books about his many explorations and adventures in the oceans around the world. Through his published exploits, he became an inspiration to many, and especially to Genie Clark. "I told my family, 'I would like to go down into the sea and be like William Beebe,'" Genie recalls.

First Genie needed to earn a college degree, if not two or three. But Genie's family could not afford to send her to college, certainly not to a private institution away from home. Fortunately, New York City had many colleges that were essentially free to its residents. In 1938, after graduating from high school at the age of 16, Genie entered the all women's Hunter College. She wanted to major in zoology and become a professional ichthyologist.

3

WHO WANTS TO BE AN ICHTHYOLOGIST?

Dissecting frogs, cats, mice, or snakes in a college biology laboratory is one thing. But doing such assignments as homework in your apartment, on the kitchen floor, is quite another. Yet, as Genie progressed through her first years at Hunter College, majoring in zoology, her study of animal anatomy seemed to know no bounds. To expose the bones of a big rat she had brought home, Genie decided to boil it in one of her Grandma Yuriko's pots. When Yuriko returned home, and lifted the lid of the bubbling "stew," she practically fainted.

Staying Awake

As Genie headed to Hunter College in the fall of 1938, her mother questioned her daughter's impending career choice. In a time when working women only had the options of being secretaries, nurses, or elementary-school teachers, her mother admonished, "Maybe you'd better take a few courses in typing and shorthand on the side. In case you don't find a job like Dr. Beebe's when you finish college, you might get a start as some famous ichthyologist's secretary."

The way Genie saw it, with homework, lab work, and her ever-encompassing hobby, she would have little time to spend taking side courses. Besides, Genie wanted to do what scientists did, not necessarily what women were supposed to do.

The 16-year-old's freshman year at college got off to a damaging start, however. Genie was suspended from school after her first semester.

Suspension is usually a punishment meted for misconduct. And, given Genie's elementary-school disciplinary problems, one might suppose that was the cause here. Nothing could be further from the truth, however. Genie studied hard her first term, but she kept falling asleep in class. It turns out she was suffering from a severe case of anemia, a condition that develops when your blood is deficient of healthy red blood cells. With rest, a special diet, and the guidance of her biology professor and new mentor, Dr. Theodora Nelson, Genie recovered and returned to college more energized than ever about becoming a marine biologist.

Cutting Up

Many students prefer hands-on learning, and Genie was no exception. She wanted to discover zoology by "doing" zoology. To Genie, lectures and books were only part of the learning process. In other words, the young undergraduate didn't just want to read about fruit flies, she wanted to breed them in bottles, follow their life cycles, and count the offspring to confirm specific laws of heredity. Fortunately, that's how they taught science at Hunter College: with a strong laboratory component.

But that didn't seem to be enough for Genie. She soon took to doing lab work as homework.

The rat incident was bad enough. But the monkey episode finally did it. It seems a local pet-shop owner, knowing Genie's interests in exploring animal innards, gave her a dead monkey. She lugged it home and stuffed the tiny primate in the refrigerator so it wouldn't smell. When Yuriko opened the freezer door, the horrifying dead monkey stared out at her. "No more dead animals in this house!" she commanded.

In the Field

While lab work gets you closer to the real thing than lectures and reading, it is through fieldwork, out among living creatures, that you can best study animal behavior. To that end, Genie took advantage of a summer study program that put her in the thick of things—literally. Along with a fellow student and friend, Norma, whom she had known since the fourth grade, Genie spent the summers of 1941 and 1942 in the cool, green woodlands of northern Michigan, studying at the University of Michigan's Biological Station.

Studying often meant bringing home snake eggs and hatching them on the camp's dining table. "Collecting fish and snakes was part of our school 'work,'" Genie later wrote. So was getting up before the birds for ornithology observations. As Genie was to grumble in her book *Lady with a Spear:* "I didn't take to it readily. It was, in fact, a dreadful moment when the alarm went off at 3:45 A.M. and Norma and I would awake hoping for the sound of a heavy rain that would cancel the class trip." Yet it couldn't have been all that bad for either of them; the following summer they both signed up for an advanced ornithology course which, because of its longer field trips, sometimes started even earlier.

Of course, being at the biological station was a lot like being at camp, too. There was plenty of time for swimming, hiking, and setting up house in a rustic cabin. It made for two fun and fulfilling summers. "We loved every minute of the field courses that gave us the chance to study animals in nature," Genie recalls. "I felt such a feeling of freedom, living in what seemed to be the wilds after being brought up completely in the city." Furthermore, there was the obvious learning benefit. Being at the station gave both students a clear advantage over others who had no opportunity to take anything but the formal schedule of courses.

Continuing Education

In 1942, at the beginning of U.S. involvement in World War II, Genie graduated from Hunter College. Unfortunately, her mother had been right: Finding a job as a zoologist, let alone as an ichthyologist, was almost impossible. So, like many people at the time, Genie went to work where the war effort needed her. She took a job as a chemist at Celanese Corporation, in their plastic-research laboratories in Newark, New Jersey.

Genie's hunger to continue her studies was intense. She applied to graduate school at Columbia University. However, the zoology department was decidedly unwelcoming. Perhaps expressing a typical attitude of the times, the department chair declared: "We could take you, but to be honest, you probably will wind up having a bunch of kids and never do anything in science." As things would turn out, the professor got it half right. Genie eventually had four children. But she would also become a world-renowned scientist. To that end, she enrolled in night school at New York University's graduate program in zoology.

Also in 1942, Genie was married to Hideo "Roy" Umaki, a dashing Japanese American man. Despite many people's prejudices against Japanese Americans at the time, Roy joined the army, became a pilot, and was shipped overseas. Genie and Roy would spend most of the remaining war years apart.

Helmet Dive

By 1946, Genie had enough of chemistry. And, with the war over, she was ready for a change. So when Dr. Carl Hubbs, a professor at the University of California's Scripps Institute of Oceanography in La Jolla, California, offered her a job as his part-time research assistant, Genie was there in a flash. She drove day and night from the East to the West Coast.

Genie soon discovered that the otherwise scholarly Dr. Hubbs was an excellent diver in addition to being a great teacher. With him, she had her first try at using a facemask. And with him, she was able to fulfill her childhood dream of walking on the sea bottom—by learning to helmet dive.

It was a beautiful, blue-skied, blue-watered Southern California day when Genie found herself on the *E. W. Scripps* research ship with Dr. Hubbs and four men studying at the Scripps Institute. The students were ready for their "water-breaking" helmet-diving lesson.

Genie aboard the E.W. Scripps (Eugenie Clark)

Before their first plunge, the Navy instructor accompanying them told each student, "Remember, it's one tug on the signal cord to say you are alright. Two tugs mean the tender should give you more line. Three tugs, and it is 'take up slack.' And four tugs means, 'Danger, pull me up fast.'"

Genie was the third diver to go down. Here is how she describes the experience in *Lady with a Spear:* "I grabbed the rope hanging beside the ladder and let myself slide down it into the heart of the kelp forest. I started walking along the sandy bottom of the sea among the waving kelp fronds that now stretched high above my head."

Everything seemed to be going fine for Genie, except for her breathing—no small matter when you are underwater. Genie continues, "I opened the air-regulating valve a little and, with relief, felt the air grow fresher. But still it seemed that breathing under two atmospheres of pressure and walking with this clumsy weight on my head was far from comfortable."

Soon, however, Genie's breathing became labored, dangerously so. She was in deep trouble. Quickly Genie gave four tugs on the cable, but nothing happened. Her eyes were burning. Her head felt numb. Her arms and legs were turning to rubber. Water had entered her helmet. Genie was about to faint.

With a splurge of strength, the novice diver slipped the heavy helmet off her head and let her buoyancy carry her upward to the surface.

On the ship, Genie was wrapped in blankets. The cook brought her a cup of hot coffee. When she tried to explain what had happened, one of the men admonished her. "Just like a girl to screw the valve the wrong way and cut off her air." But when Dr. Hubbs checked the valve, he found it was wide open. As it turns out, the air line had recently been repaired using a garden hose. The attachment had come loose. When it was repaired, Genie dived again—the same day.

An Ichthyologist's Eden

After World War II, the United States wanted to survey the fisheries in the Pacific region, specifically around the Philippine Islands. The U.S. Fish and Wildlife Service planned to send a group of marine scientists who knew something about *plectognaths,* poisonous puffer fish and the triggerfish. (Triggerfish get their name for the triggerlike mechanism controlling the large spine on the top of their head. Use of the trigger allows the fish to wedge itself into rock crevasses, where it cannot be dislodged by a predator.)

Genie seemed like the ideal candidate for the job. Her unique combination of training in chemical research at Celanese and her graduate work at Scripps clearly put Genie in the running. She applied and was accepted. In 1947, the 25-year-old graduate student was soon on her way to the Philippines, with a first stop in Hawaii.

Hawaii was as far as Genie got. As it turned out, she would be the only female scientist in the program. Some people had a problem with that. As a result of lingering resentment against Japan after World War II, the FBI wanted to check Genie's Japanese origins and connections. She never received government clearance to proceed. They hired a man to take her place.

Yet, as Genie commented in *Lady with a Spear*, "If a fish enthusiast has to be stranded in a strange place while being investigated, no place could be better than Hawaii." She spent her waiting time watching triggerfish (*humuhumu-nukunuku-a-puáa* in Hawaiian) swim around in the Waikiki Aquarium, studying the puffing apparatus of puffer fish, and enjoying the pleasures of the islands.

In Hawaii Genie was also able to see her husband for the first time in many years. Unfortunately, having spent so much time away from each other, they found their lives had grown apart. The couple would divorce two years later.

Not to Be Deterred

Having received her master's degree in 1946 from New York University, and seeing her research trip to the Philippines thwarted, Genie returned to New York to complete her formal education as an ichthyologist. To do that, she needed to earn a Ph.D.

Genie later said that the FBI might have actually done her a favor by denying her clearance in 1947. Had she spent considerable time in the Philippines, she felt, she might never have been able to return to begin the rigorous study required to complete a Ph.D. Under the guidance of Professor Myron Gordon at the American Museum of Natural History, Genie received the sponsorship she needed to pursue studies at New York University, which would include numerous "hands-on" side trips to islands such as Bimini in the West Indies. In 1950, after completing extensive research on the behavior of platies and swordtails, the same kind of fish that were in her first home aquarium, Genie would earn her doctorate degree. She was a full-fledged ichthyologist at last.

But before she would call herself Dr. Clark, Genie had some more ocean diving and fish investigating to carry out. She got her chance under a U.S. Navy sponsored program. In early 1947, the Office of Naval Research put out a call for ichthyologists interested in investigating poisonous fish in the South Pacific. Genie applied, even though she had been warned that the selection board would not be inclined to send a single woman to the South Pacific to collect fish. The usual apprehensions surfaced: The research was too rugged for a woman, there was a possibility of contracting tropical diseases, the heat might wear down a girl, and, most curious, the native fishermen may not want to dive with a woman—they would consider her presence bad luck and a taboo.

Nevertheless, Genie was accepted for the job, which she began in 1949. Her destination: the South Pacific.

4

SOUTH SEAS EXPLORATIONS

The Pacific Ocean is not only the largest body of water in the world, at 64,186,300 square miles, but it's also almost as large as the earth's other four oceans (Atlantic, Indian, Arctic, and Southern, also called the Antarctic) combined (66,875,700 square miles). The Pacific Ocean is larger than all of the land on the planet put together: It covers one-third the earth's surface.

The Pacific's average depth is more than 13,000 feet (more than two miles). Yet in its western region, near Japan and the Philippines, there are trenches that can draw you downward much further, into the abyss—and beyond. The Mariana Trench, for instance, near the island of Guam, is the deepest place in any ocean, reaching down 35,840 feet, to a point known as the Challenger Deep. At 6.8 miles below sea level, this is one deep trench. Nothing alive down there has ever seen the light of day.

In 1960 two men, Jacques Piccard and Don Walsh, were lowered into this trench in their bathyscaphe (another type of diving *submersible*, which is a miniature submarine) named the *Trieste*. As they disappeared into the perpetual blackness (where no humans have since returned), the two explorers descended past gulper eels, football fish, nautiluses, and bioluminescent hatchet fish, the latter with their gleaming bluish light organs. (More than 60 percent of deep-sea animals can make their own light to find and attract prey, confuse enemies, and communicate with members of their own species.)

Genie wasn't going to the South Pacific to deep-sea dive, however, and certainly not at those depths. She had come to explore marine life in the warm, shallow coral reefs of Micronesia, a region slightly above the equator. Consisting of 2,250 islands, the archipelago is distributed over an area nearly equal to the continental Unites States. In particular, she would be stopping at places such as Kwajalein on the eastern rim and Palau at the far west, directly north of New Guinea. Island-hopping to snorkel, dive, and spearfish, Genie was about to enter a marine biologist's paradise.

Stone Ugly

On June 17, 1949, Genie left California on a Martin Mars seaplane bound for Hawaii. With a few days layover to

Genie collects a fish from the ocean. (Eugenie Clark)

shop for supplies and visit old friends, Genie was then on her way to Kwajalein, in eastern Micronesia.

From Kwajalein Genie boarded a plane for Guam. But halfway there, the plane developed engine trouble and had to turn back. That was okay with Genie; she would spend her days waiting for another plane by spreading her new rotenone samples in local tide pools. *Rotenone* is a white, crystalline, water-insoluble substance poisonous to fish. Genie spread a few drops of rotenone on the water's surface. In no time, fish by the buckets full were stunned by rotenone's ability to prevent their gills from absorbing oxygen. They quickly floated to the surface. With volunteers, Genie dipped her nets into the water, gathering up gobies, sea horses, brown sea bass, striped damselfish, and venomous scorpions.

Speaking of poisonous fish, one that was of particular interest to Genie—yet one she wouldn't encounter directly in Kwajalein—was the ugly, rocklike stonefish, a member of the scorpionfish family that is considered the world's most venomous fish. Unlike its colorful cousin the lionfish, which is easy to spot, the stonefish has a warty, blotched body that blends in perfectly with the stony seabed. After visiting a seaman in the hospital who had been bitten by this nasty sea creature, Genie described his condition in her book *Lady with a Spear:* "He had been looking in shallow water and saw a small brown fish lying on a rock. It didn't move when he went close to it and so he reached down to pick it up with his hand. Then he felt a slight prick, which made him release the fish. In a few minutes the flesh around the wound started turning blue and three hours later his hand was swollen to the wrist and his arm was numb. Ten hours after the prick he was running a fever and the swelling had reached his shoulder."

The seaman, named Mr. Knight, survived his encounter with the stonefish. He was lucky—people have died from the sting of this pock-faced, venomous peril.

A Poison to Die For

Guam, 1,400 miles west of Kwajalein, is a U.S. possession; its natives are U.S. citizens. The 210-square-mile island (approximately three times the size of Washington, D.C.) was Genie's next stop.

Upon arrival, the young ichthyologist was ushered to her temporary housing quarters, a Quonset hut. These semicylindrical, prefabricated World War II leftovers contained everything a person would need to create a home away from home. Most of the corrugated sheet metal cabins provided a 20-by-48-foot living space, with shower, bed, a large storage area, and an abundance of charming little geckos, which are tiny lizards that scurried up the arched walls day and night.

Taking her meals, however, presented a problem for Genie. As a woman and a civilian, she did not fit within any of the various military mess hall categories. In the end, Genie wound up eating alone, being served by two Guamanian waiters in a small private dining room off the main all-male officers' quarters.

When it comes to poisonous fish, the kind that Genie was in Micronesia to study, there are two types: those that are venomous to touch and those that are poisonous to eat. The latter can have especially chilling effects. In *Lady with a Spear,* Genie describes the experience of eating a poisonous fish: "Within 30 hours after eating a poisonous fish, there is a tingling of the lips and tongue which spreads to the hands and feet and gradually develops into a numbness. . . . The victim becomes irritable, convulsive, or paralyzed. There may be joint aches, chills, fever, profuse sweating, itching, temporary blindness, painful urination, and a metallic taste in the mouth. . . . Then, there is the 'loose-tooth' sensation, causing victims to blow on ice cream to cool it or complain that their teeth are falling out."

It's no wonder, then, that Genie was a bit apprehensive when, on a bright sunny day, she found herself out on a primitive wooden outrigger canoe with two local fishermen, looking to net plenty of plectognath fishes. They caught lots of them. Then, as lunchtime approached, Quenga, the oldest fisherman, pulled out a degutted half-live squid. He dared the ichthyologist to try some.

Genie had eaten a cooked squid before, but she had never taken a bite out of a live one. She knew she was running the risk of ingesting some poison. But being fearless and brazen, she took up the challenge, as Mr. Quenga handed her the squishy squid. "I took a bite and found it wasn't half bad," Genie remembers. The two fish finders, now her new best friends, quickly finished the crusty invertebrate.

Diving with a Greek God

The Palau archipelago, covering approximately 125 miles in the western-most section of Micronesia, looks like a tropical island paradise. The islands and islets are of volcanic and coral origins. The huge coral reef structures comprise countless coral animals (polyps), each often no bigger than a pencil eraser. Joined together, the dead stony coral skeletons interlock to form barrier, fringe, and

During her time in Palau, Genie learned to fish with a spear.
(Eugenie Clark)

atoll reefs. In and around these coral reef habitats swim and cling an incredible diversity of coral, fish, and other multicolored marine animals, such as mollusks and crustaceans. Although coral reefs make up less than one percent of the entire ocean seafloor, these "rainforests of the ocean" are inhabited by approximately 25 percent of all known marine species (a third of all fish species). It is estimated that upward of 15,000 live among the spectacular coral Eden of Palau.

It was here, on the island of Koror, that Genie would now make her Pacific headquarters. It is also where she met Siakong, a rough and sometimes violent man who happened to be, according to legend (which he helped promote), the best spear fisherman in the world.

Siakong was over 50 years old when Genie met him. When he wore a small loincloth and homemade goggles, however, his build and strength transformed him from a brute to something more like a Greek god. He would teach Genie much about spear diving, net throwing, and Palau's underwater turquoise waters.

Siakong's spears were of the old-fashioned variety, strictly homemade. About 12 feet long, their bamboo shafts were tipped with metal heads. They were light enough to float to the surface, should one be lost in a throw.

When Genie was finally ready to try her arm at spear fishing, she dove for triggerfish with Siakong. When she first spotted one, however, it wedged itself in between two rocks. As Genie speared the fish, she then attempted to withdraw it from between the rocks. All she wound up doing was shredding her specimen. True to its name, the fish had "triggered" its dorsal fin to "spring" out, thus locking itself in its hiding place. No amount of pushing or pulling could lower the spine, it would seem.

Siakong, however, showed Genie how to defeat the fish's ingenious mechanism. When it was his turn to chase a triggerfish, he reached in behind the trapped fish and pressed its releaser "button." The fin collapsed, and out came the bewildered vertebrate.

Near the end of her Palau visit, Siakong assured Genie he would always be around should she ever return. "I'll still be a good fisherman when I am 80," he boasted to her. But a few years later Genie learned that Siakong, after being released from a long stint in jail, went on a fishing trip and never returned. He took a deep dive after a turtle and never came up again. Today, the grandchildren of his relatives and friends keep Siakong's legend alive.

Native Royalty

Genie's purpose for coming to the South Pacific was to both study and collect fish, particularly the poisonous varieties, those toxic to eat and to touch. But the South Seas native people were of interest to her, too. Fais Island, about 350 miles east of Palau, would provide a curious study in human behavior, particularly with regard to the role of women.

As Genie walked about the island, shaking hands and glancing around, she came upon a row of chieftains sitting cross-legged in front of a large grass-covered *abai*, or hut. The chiefs could be distinguished from the island's ordinary "workers" by their bulging bellies, fat bodies, and heavily tattooed, smoothly rounded and relaxed limbs. As Genie sat among the island royalty, she noticed the apparent absence of women. None seemed to be on the island. Eventually, however, a few women began to appear, approaching her

Genie sits among tribal chiefs on Fais Island. (Eugenie Clark)

and the chiefs in a crouched-over position, with their backs almost parallel to the ground. It seemed that the island's customs required that women approach men, particularly those of royal rank, in such a manner. Genie, being a foreigner, was allowed to forgo what would be, in any Western society, an unacceptable indignity.

With her South Pacific adventures about to conclude, Genie could now ask herself whether anyone's initial apprehensions about her being a woman and traveling alone in the region were justified. Perhaps she had been lucky, Genie thought. There was only one instance worth noting, when a drunken sailor chased her along the beach on a somewhat out of the way Pacific island. She outran him. As Genie was later to observe in her book *Lady with a Spear*, it's all in how you present yourself. "I can't help believing," she wrote, "that a man in his right mind (whether he be a South Sea islander, a sailor in the U.S. Navy, or any stranger) respects a woman who does not invite trouble and who makes it clear she is just trying to do her work."

Her work done, it was now time for Genie to return home, where she encountered a new love beyond her scientific calling—a Greek medical doctor by the name of Ilias Themistokles Papakonstantinou. Soon after meeting Ilias, Genie declared, "He had the personality that could tempt a female ichthyologist's interests away from fish."

5

A SEA TO SEE

At 225 miles wide, 1,450 miles long, and, at places, more than a mile deep, the Red Sea is like a huge water-filled rift separating the Arabian Peninsula from the African Continent. It is practically landlocked. A tiny opening at the north provides access to the Mediterranean Sea, through the Suez Canal. The 17-mile-wide straits of Bab el Mandeb, in the south, open to the Arabian Sea.

Though less than 100 miles separate the Red Sea from its northern neighbor, the Mediterranean, the latter is considered temperate, while the former is tropical. The result is that Red Sea marine life is similar to that found in the Indo-Pacific Oceans. As Genie observes in *Lady with a Spear* (published in 1953): "The blenny that skips around the tide pools of Hawaii does the same along the Red Sea; the commonest poisonous puffer fish in Hawaii offers the same danger in the Red Sea."

It was these marine similarities that allowed Genie, in 1950, to make her case for a Fulbright scholarship, one that would send her to the Middle East to compare what could be found in the Red Sea to that of the Pacific Ocean. That virtually no scientific report had been made on the region's fish in more than 70 years added weight to her quest. Genie sent in her proposal, and, sure enough, it was accepted.

Understanding and Support

Although Genie was excited about her new career development, she might have worried about how such a separation might affect her new romantic relationship. But as Genie was to discover, Ilias was a young doctor who showed a genuine interest in her work, more so than any other man she had dated. He seemed to hold no resentment against the studies that absorbed her. Besides, being Greek and a doctor, Ilias had a distinct advantage to bring to the relationship: He could pronounce and understand all of the scientific names Genie was always throwing around in conversation.

And, indeed, the two often spent "date" nights doing just that. "There were evenings," Genie writes, "when I was pressed for time, when our 'date' consisted of translating a German ichthyological article or my calling out numbers to him and his running a calculating machine while we figured out the data on my experimental work at the Department of Animal Behavior."

Thus, Genie couldn't really complain when she spent a whole evening waiting in the lobby of St. Clare's Hospital for Ilias to finish a "twenty minute" appendectomy.

When the Fulbright scholarship came through, it wasn't surprising, therefore, that Ilias gave his full support. "That sounds terrific," he told her. "Studying fish in the Red Sea! And you'll be able to stop off and visit my parents in Athens."

On Christmas Eve, 1950, Genie arrived in Cairo. Two weeks later, she was at the little Marine Biological Station

Genie hunts for fish using a speargun. (Eugenie Clark)

at Ghardaqa, an isolated spot at the eastern edge of the Libyan Desert, where barren sand meets the blue waters of the Red Sea.

Culture Shock

Ghardaqa, a village four miles from the Marine Biological Station, is in Egypt, as much a Muslim country in 1950 as it is today. From her front porch at the laboratory, Genie could see Islamic worshipers going down to the sea and washing themselves before entering the local mosque to pray.

The fishermen, sailors, and divers with whom Genie dealt spoke no English or French—only Arabic. Thus, Genie needed to learn Arabic, or at least enough to get by.

Genie took to Arabic enthusiastically, if not easily. She found Arabic writing, which moves from right to left on the page, a delight to learn. She loved the decorative nature of the script and quickly mastered the alphabet. Still, Arabic is a tough language for a Westerner to conquer. Luckily, as time went on, Genie found the locals more than willing to give plenty of slack with her rough pronunciations and unladylike expressions. Her broken Arabic was to remain broken throughout her stay.

An unveiled woman, wearing a bathing suit and out fishing and swimming with men, was harder for the villagers to accept, however—at least at first. Most women in

Ghardaqa disapproved. Instead of turning away from Genie on the dusty streets, the women gradually began answering her greetings. And, eventually, in the privacy of their homes, where the veils came off, the women of Ghardaqa chatted with Genie, sharing stories and showering her with gifts of perfume.

Busy Days and Wedding Bells

Throughout her stay in Ghardaqa, Genie claims she was never lonely. And, given all that the ichthyologist had to do, one could see why she wouldn't be.

At times, Genie would spend an entire day out at sea. That was the fun part. As with all jobs, however, there are routine tasks to be carried out, too. That is usually the least exciting part. Genie's work was no exception

The sorting and cataloging of the day's catch had to be done almost immediately after a return to the lab. Living specimens needed to be placed in the various aquariums and arranged in groups that would get along together.

As Genie was to observe later on, first encounters of fish in an aquarium can be particularly interesting to watch. In one instance, she observed a puffer fish that, upon being dropped into an aquarium, quickly went from a dull olive color to a display of bright gold around its eyes, all in a flash. And it never did it again. Perhaps it was a warning to other fish, saying, "I am here, stay away from me." Or there was the puffer that nonchalantly swam past a tiny damselfish for the first and only time. After that, the puffer learned to keep away from the aggressive little attacker. As with all animal life, marine life is about establishing territory and setting boundaries, often by not displaying a timid demeanor. It is about survival.

If Genie was indeed lonely at times, that loneliness ended one day in June when Ilias arrived, having been able to take a few weeks off from his busy work. Genie went to Cairo to meet him. They were married in a Greek Orthodox Church near the Khan el-Khalili bazaar.

The marriage ceremony was conducted entirely in Greek. Not knowing Greek, Genie couldn't follow any of it, including instructions that were directed to her. So, when the priest officiating the ceremony brought Ilias's ring within an inch of Genie's mouth and nodded to her, she responded as she had been taught during her own communion ceremonies. Genie opened her mouth wide, stuck out her tongue, and waited for the priest to place the wafer upon it.

Shocked, the stricken priest withdrew the ring quickly. "You only have to kiss it," he admonished Genie. And, when the bible was passed around a bit later, the priest didn't take any chances. "Don't try to eat it, just kiss it," he advised.

Honeymooning with the Sharks

There are sharks in the Red Sea—plenty of them. One species, the nurse shark, is harmless. In fact, Genie took a picture of Ilias in a shallow pool with seven nurse sharks swimming around him, each longer than the doctor. Being as gentle as the whale shark, nurse sharks can grow to be 10 feet long.

The mako, tiger, and hammerhead sharks, also found in the Red Sea, are not so docile, however. It is best to stay clear when swimming with these predators.

Take the hammerhead, for example. Not only is it menacing, but it is also one of the strangest looking creatures in the ocean. No one knows quite why its head spreads out to half its length, with eyes and nostrils on both sides. The shark swings this odd "growth" back and forth constantly, all the better to see a wide expanse and detect as many smells as possible. If that weren't enough to give it a search-and-destroy advantage, the hammerhead's "hammer" is also packed with what is known as the ampullae of Lorenzini, pores that can sense electrical signals emanating from fish, even those that are hidden. All the local fishermen at Ghardaqa agreed: The hammerhead shark is highly dangerous.

Genie and Ilias never encountered a hammerhead on their honeymoon, to the doctor's disappointment, evidently. One day the newlyweds were out and about in a

Throughout her career, Genie has gone on many diving and research expeditions around the world. (James L. Stanfield/ National Geographic Image Archive)

shallow bay. Ilias was blissfully diving among the colorful corals, his sparkling new white sneakers looking, from a distance, like two little fishes—nice bait for a barracuda.

As Ilias swam about, churning bubbles, he was unknowingly swimming right into a barracuda's path. Though not dangerous, barracuda certainly appear threatening. Ilias didn't know this, however, and he scrambled aboard the boat. When informed by Genie that it wasn't a shark chasing him, but "merely" a barracuda, Ilias was disappointed. He thought a shark attack would have made his honeymoon complete.

6

SHARK STUDIES

By 1954, Genie was again in New York, living with Ilias and their two children, Hera and Aya. It was at this time that she accepted an invitation from Anne and William Vanderbilt to give a lecture in Englewood, Florida. But there was more to the invitation than met the eye. Upon arrival, Genie was to receive an offer that few marine biologists would refuse.

A Lab of Her Own

The Vanderbilts' 10-year-old son, Bill Jr., had a bedroom full of aquariums, as had Genie at his age, and the boy's parents were fascinated with their son's hobby. The Vanderbilts, who owned a 36,000-acre tract of land in the area, wanted to know if Genie would be willing to move down to Florida and start her own marine laboratory.

The Vanderbilts would help financially to get things started.

Today, there are dozens of marine labs around the world. Some, such as the Marine Biological Laboratory and the Woods Hole Oceanographic Institution in Woods Hole, Massachusetts, or the Scripps Institution of Oceanography in La Jolla, California, are huge, well-funded, internationally recognized research institutions associated with major universities. But the lab that Genie was asked to inaugurate 50 years ago would be, to say the least, a more modest undertaking.

Genie agreed to give it a try. Although she had her doubts about her ability to give the new laboratory the direction it needed to become a useful and respected organization, and not just a place for her to satisfy her own curiosities about fish, she simply couldn't pass up the opportunity to create a lab of her own.

The following year, Genie opened the Cape Haze Marine Laboratory, becoming its first director. Her enthusiasm was expressed best when she wrote in *The Lady and the Sharks*, "I felt incredibly lucky with my first full-time job, doing what I always wanted to do most—study fish—with everything all in one place, collecting grounds, a laboratory, and my home and family, who liked our new life in Florida as much as I did."

Genie would remain as director until 1967.

Fish in a Jar

When Ilias reestablished his medical practice in Florida in early 1955, the whole Clark family was together again, far from often-frigid New York. The Vanderbilts had prepared a small wooden building, 12-by-20 feet, constructed on skids, to house the lab's headquarters at the shore of Gasparilla Sound. Not long after, a 40-by-70-foot stockaded pen was built adjacent to the lab's dock. It was to hold live sharks, all the better to study their behavior and perform experiments.

Almost from its inception, the lab not only attracted sharks, but it also attracted children, particularly in the summer. One such kid, Carey Winfrey, was only 13 years old, yet he was able to convince his father to let him live alone in a nearby motel while he kept himself busy volunteering at the lab. Here, Carey spent time boiling the fish heads, cleaning the dozens of bones that fell apart in their complex skulls, and then gluing them back together again. He wouldn't be the last kid to take to the Cape Haze Marine Laboratory, with all its activity-oriented wonders.

Spending summers in a hot lab dissecting fish wasn't Genie's idea of a great time, however. She wanted to get in the water where she could dive, stay cool, and study marine creatures in their natural environment. Besides, she needed to catch fish for the lab.

Soon enough, Genie was out swimming in the colorful reef near Boca Grande Pass, trying to capture fish in a glass jar. It wasn't easy.

First, she had to make a fact-finding dive to study the fishes' habits and movements. Then she chased a fish with a stick, studying the way it moved about in its territory and where its favorite hiding places were. After figuring out the fish's movements, she would plant an open glass jar in what she hoped would be its direct path. Finally, if she could manage to hold her breath, Genie let her free hand follow behind the fish and close the jar as

Genie has always felt most comfortable doing what she loves best: diving and studying ocean life. (James L. Stanfield/ National Geographic Image Archive)

the unsuspecting swimming vertebrate entered. After much diving and practice, Genie got pretty good at it.

Shark Conditioning

For the longest time, many people (a few marine biologists among them) thought that sharks were just simple-minded but highly efficient killing machines. To be sure, some of the estimated 400 shark species are ruthless predators.

Indeed, sand tiger sharks are downright cannibalistic. Not only are they born to kill, but they are born having *already* killed. These sharks develop from fertilized eggs inside their mother and remain inside her body after they are hatched. Only two will eventually emerge, one from each side of their mother's reproductive organs. What happens to the rest of the eggs and embryos? You guessed it—the two juvenile "winners" eat them. When there is nothing left to feed on, the two survivors break from their mother. Already seasoned killers, they are ready to devour anew with their daggerlike teeth.

Although sharks seem to have a one-track mind when it comes to their prey, Genie and other marine biologists suspected they are far from being dumb creatures. To that end, Genie wanted to see if sharks could be taught a lesson or two, or in other words, be trained as a dog might be.

In 1958, at the encouragement of visiting professor Dr. Lester Aronson, Genie began developing plans to place her sharks into a modified Skinner Box. Such a box, named after its inventor, noted behaviorist B. F. Skinner, uses positive and negative reinforcement to model behavior in small steps that allow a subject to learn complex actions. The Skinner Box is a device that uses a reward system to condition animals to behave in a prescribed way. For example, a rat will be placed inside the box. A stimulus, like a light bulb turning on, is then introduced. When the rat responds to the stimulus—by pushing a lever inside the box, for instance—it is rewarded with a food pellet. Birds and rats were the typical trial subjects for the Skinner Box. No one had tried such experiments with sharks.

Dr. Aronson suggested that Genie and her volunteers place a target in the water and train a shark to take a piece of mullet from the target in such a way that the shark would bump its nose against it. As a result, a bell would ring. After a time, the shark might associate the target with food. The shark would then press the target and ring the bell even when the food was no longer presented with the target. The experimenters would use the feeding end of the lab's shark pen as a kind of Skinner Box.

The Bell Tolls

By the end of September 1958, Genie and her crew were ready to begin a strict training program with her lemon sharks. They began by putting a target in the water for a maximum of 20 minutes. They fed the sharks in front of the target, dangling a piece of mullet from a string. After a few days, the shark was lured in so close that in order to get food in its mouth, it was forced to press its nose against the target.

After six weeks of feeding the sharks with the target in front of the food, the lab was ready for the big test. Genie put the target in the water at the appointed time but with no food in front of it. Here is how she describes a male lemon shark's reaction to the target: "Finally, he nuzzled the empty target hard enough to set off the automatic bell, and we quickly tossed out a reward piece of food wrapped in confetti string that hit the water with a splash just to the left of the target. The shark quickly grabbed the food, cutting the string with his teeth."

Clearly, the shark in Genie's experiment had associated pressing the target with getting his food. The lab's staff had succeeded in "instrumentally conditioning" a lemon shark. In the coming months and years, more experiments would confirm that sharks were indeed a lot smarter than had previously been thought.

Leaving the Lab

As the years went by, Genie began to notice that her job as lab director was changing. It had gone from three-fourths research and one-fourth paper work to just the opposite. This was not a happy trend for Genie. She was a diver and an ichthyologist first. Administration was not Genie's strong point, nor her main interest.

Even the lab's move to new facilities in 1960 did not help to reinvigorate Genie. Her mother had died in the summer of 1959, from a brain hemorrhage. Genie was crushed. Even setting the world's record for freshwater diving that year failed to lift her spirits. She lost interest in her work. Finally, she wrote a letter of resignation to the Vanderbilts, telling them that she could no longer devote the necessary time to the lab but said that she would stay until a new director could take over.

Genie actually remained, in one manner or another, as director for another five years. At times she tried working part time. They hired a full-time business manager, which freed Genie to spend at least some time doing what she loved most: riding sea turtles and swimming with manta rays, for instance. And the lab expanded. By 1965, it had grown from a field station to a major research center.

But Genie's personal life had changed, too. Though she now had four children, her marriage to Ilias had come to an end in early 1966. Genie decided to move north with her children, to accept a teaching position at the University of Maryland. She was, once again, to begin a new chapter in her life. Genie had much more to learn and discover, as an ichthyologist specializing in shark studies, as a college professor, and, to a growing extent, as a media celebrity in her field.

Genie and a colleague prepare equipment before fishing for sharks in Sagami Bay, Japan. (Paul Chesley/National Geographic Image Archive)

7

ROYAL VISITOR

Most of us have received a truly strange gift at least once in our lifetime. But how about a small, well-trained, live nurse shark? In the summer of 1965, Genie, at age 43, was about to make her first trip to Japan. Her notoriety as an ichthyologist, with a growing expertise in shark behavior, had crossed national boundaries. Crown Prince of Japan Akihito, who was also an ichthyologist himself, heard of Genie's behavioral research at the Cape Haze Marine Laboratory and invited her to visit him at the Royal Palace. Some of Genie's Japanese friends told her it would be customary for her to bring a gift. What better present than one of her target-pushing sharks?

Getting a shark from Florida to Japan is no easy matter. Special agents were assigned to help with the special delivery at transfer points in Tampa, Los Angeles, and Honolulu. The shark, swimming in a carrying box no bigger than a hatbox, got an extra seat at no charge. At the Tokyo airport, a special truck with a built-in aquarium tank was standing by for the pickup.

A large party gathered to await the royal visitor. As Genie describes it in *The Lady and the Sharks*: "In the midst of a huge welcoming party, including friends, scientists, professors, newspaper reporters, TV cameras, and gawkers, we dumped the little shark that had traveled in a 'hatbox' halfway around the world into a giant aquarium to transport him away."

A Royal Performance

On top of a table in a room at the palace, in a low 4-by-6-foot aquarium, the visiting shark now swam. As the prince entered, a servant stood by holding a beautiful platter with slices of raw lobster arranged in the shape of an expanding flower. All was ready for the shark's performance.

A tiny target had been placed in the aquarium. Sure enough, almost on command, the shark pushed the small, square target with its nose. He was instantly rewarded with a slice of lobster that the servant placed within easy grasp. Camera strobes flashed, as reporters scurried about the room.

After the show, the prince took Genie on a tour of his laboratory rooms and aquariums. It was here that Akihito confessed that he didn't like to eat fish, only to study and collect them. Furthermore, the prince told her he had never learned to skin dive—not once had he looked underwater through a facemask.

That oversight was to be rectified, however, two years later, when the prince was passing through Miami, returning from a trip to South America. Sure enough, at the prince's request, Genie took him and his entire entourage down to the sea at 5:00 A.M. to go skin diving. As the prince took his first snorkel dive, his attendants, all wearing shirts and ties, their trousers rolled up, stood by on the shore, their drawn faces showing their anxiety. The prince caught a prize *Bathygobius soporator* (also called a Frillfin goby). His trip was a success.

A New Mystery

In 1969 Genie published her second book, *The Lady and the Sharks*, which detailed her 12 years as the Cape Haze Marine Laboratory Director. The book sold quite well and enhanced and highlighted Genie's expanding role in shark studies.

It was also around this time that a new and mysterious aspect of shark behavior captured Genie's interest. Conventional wisdom said that sharks must always stay in motion to breathe, but she was about to discover sharks that seemed to defy that theory.

Many sharks have relatively weak gill muscles. As a result, they must continuously swim with their mouths open to extract oxygen from the water as it passes over their gills. Using *ram ventilation,* such sharks stay in motion most of the time.

Other sharks have a *gill pump,* a set of muscles that suck in water and push it past their gills. They can stay still while continuously gathering oxygen. Of the two methods, ram ventilation and gill pumping, the latter requires a lot more work, expending considerably more energy.

Thus, imagine Genie's surprise when a young Mexican lobster fisherman, Carlos Garcia, told her about underwater caves off the Yucatan peninsula where supposedly man-eating requiem sharks lie comatose for hours, seeming to pump water over their gills instead of just swimming about the sea.

When Carlos had first found the inactive sharks, he assumed they were dead. But not so: The sharks were alive, if not strangely narcotized. How, why, would the sharks act so lethargic? Genie, ever ready to dive, had to find out more about these "sleeping" sharks herself.

Close Encounters

Under the sponsorship of the National Geographic Society, Mexican government, and, at times, the Explorers Club, Genie assembled a research team. Her main assistant was

Genie gets up close and personal with a bull shark. (Emory Kristof/National Geographic Image Archive)

Anita George, one of her students at the University of Maryland. Together the two would come face-to-face with a potentially deadly requiem shark.

In early 1974, Genie and Anita were followed by a huge, pregnant requiem into an underwater cavern off the Mexican coast. Suddenly, the shark turned and swam toward them. For reasons not fully understood to this day—maybe it was the divers' underwater movie lights or the tranquilizing influences of the water—the shark stopped abruptly, just two feet in front of the spellbound divers. Here is how Genie describes the encounter, in an

April 1975 *National Geographic* article: "I could see every detail—even, on the snout, the pattern of the ampullae of Lorenzini. . . . Her eyes were open: the nictitating membranes didn't even blink in the strong light. Her mouth opened and closed rhythmically."

Yet the requiem shark, a principle man-eater, remained on good behavior. It settled back, remained stationary, and fell into a sleeplike state. Genie called the encounter one of the truly unforgettable moments in her life.

After the excitement of this close encounter died down, the question remained: Why did these sharks seem to sleep? Why would predatory sharks want to hide in a cave for hours on end?

As the summer of 1974 wore on, Genie, with her assistants (her daughter, Aya, among them), sought answers by measuring depth, water temperature, oxygen content, salinity, and speed and direction of currents in the caves. Most significant, the oxygen meter they used showed high readings even in the deepest dead-end parts of the caverns they were exploring. This above-normal amount of oxygen in the water probably allowed the sharks to remain inactive for hours on end.

Also, instruments showed lower salinity and higher acidity and carbon-dioxide content than water outside the caves. Furthermore, one of Genie's assistants, Michael Resio, theorized that the "sleeping" sharks could be experiencing a pleasure stimulus from the effects of various physical and chemical conditions in the cave. Perhaps, according to Resio's theory, "The coming together of fresh water and salt water in the caves creates electromagnetic fields, and sharks exposed to this phenomenon may get 'high,' much as humans are affected by alcohol. . . ."

All in all, Genie and her team logged 99 dives in the region, on 28 of which they saw sharks. In seven cases, the sharks were "sleeping," though, of course, they actually remained conscious and aware of activity around them. Since Genie's dives in the Yucatan caves, other similar shark dormitories have been discovered. The research into this strange phenomenon continues.

In Search of Shark Repellent

Its scientific name is *Pardachirus marmoratus.* It looks like a typical flounder, a flatfish that you would buy in the supermarket. While some people eat the fish after it is well cooked, most marine species, including sharks, wouldn't touch it. Known more generally as the *Moses sole,* this fish secretes a lethally toxic, milky poison from glands along its dorsal and anal fins. Marine biologists wondered: If the fish can repel a shark, could the toxin it carries possibly act as a shark repellent? In 1973, Genie had returned to the Red Sea, under the sponsorship of the National Geographic Society, to find out.

This time she was accompanied not only by her long-time photographer, David Doubilet, but also by Gail Weinmann, a medical student; Willard Cook, a high-school senior; and Niki, her 14-year-old son.

One test the group performed early on was to place but one-part of the milky poison in five thousand parts seawater in the vicinity of many small fish species, including the hardy damselfish. All died within minutes.

Next, the team tried exposing a moray eel to the toxin. The eel could not lay a tooth on the Moses sole. After approaching, it writhed backward in a hurried escape.

The team thought that surely a vicious barracuda would not be deterred by the poison. But not so. As Genie recounts in a November 1974 article in *National Geographic*, "I could have counted the barracuda's teeth as it charged straight toward the *Pardachirus* in my hand. But at the last possible moment it stopped cold, shook its head, and shot away. Its teeth never touched us!"

Yet the biggest test still had to be made. Would the Moses sole actually repel a shark? After repeated tests, it was clear that the answer is yes. Genie, on numerous trips to the Red Sea, tried to feed Moses soles to sharks. They would approach, open their gaping mouths, and—freeze. The sharks would not take a bite.

Obviously, it was time to think of the Moses sole's milky toxin as a possible shark repellent. Genie was hopeful. As she declared in the *National Geographic* article: "I look forward to the day when research on *Pardachirus* and its potent toxin has advanced to allow this scenario: I get into my wet suit and spray it with the synthesized poison of the Moses sole. Then I dive in and swim at ease among the sharks, exempt from concern that these old friends may make me an item in their diet."

Unfortunately, even today, no such repellent exists. But thanks to the groundbreaking work that Genie started, research continues.

Teacher Extraordinary

During the 1970s, Genie had settled comfortably into her role as college professor at the University of Maryland. She was a popular teacher in the department of zoology. Genie showed uninhibited enthusiasm for her subject. She knew that teaching was not about what teachers teach, but what students learn. And Genie never forgot what it was like to be a novice—that is, she understood how intimidating zoology might seem to first-year students. As a result of her excellent teaching, major research projects, and numerous travels and speaking engagements, Genie was awarded a full professorship in 1973.

During this time, Genie visited more than 20 countries, often taking along friends, colleagues, graduate students, and even her children. Hera, Aya, Tak, and Niki, though

In addition to her active field research, Genie has been a respected teacher and lecturer for many years. (James L. Stanfield/National Geographic Image Archive)

living with their father in Florida, often accompanied their mother on various expeditions.

Genie was also becoming a TV personality. She consulted and appeared in a *National Geographic* special called *The Sharks.* It became one of the most popular shows ever seen on public television.

A Ride Like No Other

In 1981, Genie was once again in the water, this time off the coast of Baja, California. She was about to take the ride of a lifetime, but it wasn't on a horse, a camel, or even an elephant: Genie was about to ride a shark.

It was in the summer of 1981, and Genie, along with three other divers, was scuba diving in Mexican waters, off lower California. All of a sudden, they came head-to-head with the mouth of a whale shark, big enough, with its cavernous opening, to swallow all four divers whole.

As the shark veered sharply to the right, presenting its massive profile, Genie "took in" the 13-ton, 40-foot-long, plankton-eating behemoth. She quickly swam to its side, around its massive pectoral fin, and made her way to the great dorsal fin at the top. The shark was swimming at three knots, too fast for Genie to keep up. Her fellow divers had already backed away. But Genie wanted to stay with the giant, one of the largest whale sharks she had ever seen. There was only way she could do that. She would have to hitch a ride.

And that she did. Here is how she recounts her incredible journey, one few had taken before, in an August 1981, *National Geographic* article: "I had to find a handhold fast. . . . Groping at the base of the dorsal fin along its trailing edge, I discovered a soft cavity like an armpit and promptly dug my fingers into it. Then we were off on a submarine voyage down the coast of Baja, California."

Eventually, Genie was thrown off her swimming "bus," having retreated to the base of its immense tail. As she continues: "Now, instead of being towed smoothly forward I was swooshed from side to side. I tumbled off, catapulted by the whiplash movement of its tail, which came back and slapped me once. My scuba tank had already come loose, my facemask fell around my neck, and one flipper came off. I replaced the mask and got a last look at the shark as it began to dive."

For Genie, her first shark ride was the high point in a lifelong study of these graceful, fascinating creatures. Yet

A giant whale shark (Landov)

it was not the culmination. Far from it. Genie had a lot more to explore and discover. But to do so, she would require a new method of exploration, one that would, ironically, take her back to the days of the bathysphere and the bathyscaphe. Genie was about to make her first submersible dive.

8

GOING DEEP

Genie considers herself a diver first, an ichthyologist second. As a result, she has experienced decades of joy and fulfillment while swimming in the world's oceans and seas. Unfortunately, Genie has also witnessed her share of diving tragedies. One such incident occurred when Tommy Romans, an 18-year-old student and regular at the Cape Haze Marine Laboratory, died while trying to dive 100 feet while holding his breath.

Despite the very real risks of diving, marine biologists, and ichthyologists in particular, must go where marine life exists. Genie knew this from childhood, when, while visiting the Battery Park Aquarium, she first dreamed of swimming with sharks.

Beyond Scuba Diving

During Genie's first helmet dive, in 1946, she nearly drowned when her air hose broke. Yet Genie got right back in the water, undeterred. She continued to make helmet

Despite her fame as an ichthyologist, Genie considers herself first and foremost a diver. (Paul Chesley/National Geographic Image Archive)

dives until a better method, scuba (which stands for *self-contained underwater breathing apparatus*), came along.

Of course, even before there was scuba, there was snorkeling. Using a plastic tube called a snorkel, a diver can take a big breath, dive down, and stay submerged for up to a minute or two.

But to breathe underwater, sometimes for hours on end, divers need to carry a tank of compressed air on their backs, like a backpack. Unlike snorkeling, scuba diving requires training and preparation.

Genie has spent a good part of her life scuba diving, beginning soon after the apparatus became commercially available in 1952. Nonetheless, even with scuba gear, you can go only so deep—230 feet being the maximum safe depth, though the record dive is 350 feet. If marine biologists want to go really deep—from 650 to 6,500 feet and beyond—they need more than a scuba tank. They must dive in a submersible.

For example, although a French-U.S. team used remote-controlled video equipment to first discover the wreck of the *Titanic* in 1985, it was with submersibles that the sunken ship was extensively explored. The French sub *Nautile* reached the *Titanic* first, 2.3 miles down. The *Nautile* has extra thick, curved Plexiglas portholes that actually flatten on the dive due to the immense pressure at the *Titanic*'s depths. The submersible and its three-person crew took an hour and a half to reach the famed ship that went down in icy North Atlantic waters in 1912, after hitting an iceberg.

For marine biologists like Genie, exploring the underwater world in a submersible meant taking up where Beebe, in his bathysphere, and Piccard and Walsh, in the *Trieste*, had left off.

Going Deep at Last

In 1986, at age 64, Genie got her chance to descend well beyond scuba range with her first submersible dive in the three-person craft *Pisces VI*. Off Bermuda's mid-Atlantic seamount, the *Pisces VI*, piloted by Tim Marzolf, dove 2,000 feet through the shark-infested waters to the ocean floor. Though the *Pisces VI* was far more maneuverable than the bathysphere that Beebe took down in the same region more than 50 years prior, this sub, like most submersibles, made lots of noise. The clamor seemed to frighten away the very creatures that Genie and Tim had come to observe.

To conquer the noise problem, Emory Kristof had developed a technique that used the sub as a *blind*—a place of concealment—like in duck hunting. He would set the *Pisces VI* on the bottom, put out some bait, take a nap, and see what came around. On Genie and Tim's first dive, a 12-foot-long six-gill shark swam out of the dark and made

Television cameras film Genie as she examines a shark.
(National Geographic Society)

off with the bait. Six gills are rare in a shark; five is the norm. Thanks to this dive, and subsequent submersible descents, more such discoveries were to come.

Indeed, Genie, over the next few years, was to make more than 70 submersible dives, some as deep as 12,000 feet. Even in her late 60s, she was as active as ever.

ROVs, the New Submersibles

Going into the ocean's depths in a submersible is the latest rage for tourists: Two million passengers did it in 2003. However, taking down such a vehicle for research purposes is getting harder to do. It's too expensive. For Genie, as for many other scientists, it wasn't just advancing age that eventually halted such dives. Availability and access to the submersibles was becoming prohibitive.

Since the mid-1950s, an estimated 140 commercial and scientific manned submersibles have been built. Yet only about 40 are still operating, 12 of which are in the United States. The U.S. government hasn't fitted a new research submarine in more than 30 years.

Of course, one could build his or her own "personal" sub and go exploring. Many have done just that. According to John Newman, director of Underwater Vehicles, a consulting and chartering company in Vancouver, Canada, "Having one is like being in your own aquarium." But designing and building such homemade submersibles requires considerable skill, ingenuity, and money. As Jon Wallace, a software engineer who studies underwater craft in his spare time, put it, "Anyone can build a sub to go down in, but if you want to come back up alive, you have to put some thought into it."

For safety and cost reasons, most underwater research is now being done by remote-operated vehicles (ROVs). ROVs are connected to a mother ship by long cables. Cameras transmit images to operators on the ship above. The topside ship's crew steers the vehicle remotely, as though they were in it.

Still Active

The costly nature of submersible exploration did not keep Genie out of the water altogether, however. After retiring from the University of Maryland in 1992, she continued to teach part time, write, and lead research excursions. As the new millennium began, she led such expeditions to the South Pacific and La Paz, Mexico.

In 1997, Genie got married again, this time to an old friend, Henry Yoshinobu Kon.

In early 2004, Genie was still at work at the Mote Marine Laboratory (formerly the Cape Haze Marine Laboratory), in Sarasota, Florida. Her lifelong friend, Norma, was still working with her, helping to classify and catalog marine life.

Genie has often been seen as a woman ahead of her time, an inspiration to girls seeking to go where only men have gone before. Today, due in no small part to her efforts, marine biology is as much a woman's career as it is a man's. Yet Genie has an interesting perspective on this matter. In 1979, she told *Ms.* magazine: "In the beginning, I wanted to enter what was essentially a man's field. I wanted to prove I could do it. Then I found that when I did as well as men in the field, I got more credit for my work because I am a woman, which seems unfair."

Credit, to be sure, Genie has received plenty of. A list of her achievements—teaching, writing, research, and awards —runs 25 pages. She has lived an accomplished life.

Throughout, though, she has maintained her fascination with the animal that she will forever be identified with—the shark. "When a shark looks right into my eyes and I look at it," she says, "I just feel I am with one of the most magnificent creatures in the world."

Yet for Genie, perhaps the greatest joy is seeing members of her own family following in her footsteps. Her daughter Hera pursued a Ph.D. and worked, along with her marine archeologist husband, at the Mote Laboratory. Genie's daughter Aya is a captain for a major airline. Her son Tak is a photographer and diver. And Niki, Genie's

Genie in her office at the University of Maryland
(Bev Rodgerson)

youngest son, works for Cirque du Soleil, in Las Vegas, as the show's underwater coordinator.

Genie's grandchild, Eli, is for sure her greatest pride. In 1996, at age five, Eli was playing in the ocean when a whale shark swam under him. As Genie relates the story: "With his first roll of film, using a throw-away camera, Eli took pictures of the shark, from head to tail, end to end. *National Geographic* magazine actually published the pictures." In 2004, Eli received his junior scuba certificate.

And as for Genie, to celebrate her 82nd birthday, in 2004, she planned an activity that was only in keeping with her lifelong love of the sea: a six-week diving expedition in Papua, New Guinea. There she would continue her studies, this time looking into strange fish that tunnel under coral reefs.

TIME LINE

1922 Born May 4 in New York

1931 Begins visits to Battery Park Aquarium (New York)

1938 Graduates from high school at 16; enters Hunter College

1942 Receives bachelor's degree in zoology from Hunter College; marries Roy Umaki

1946 Receives master's degree in zoology from New York University (NYU); works with Carl Hubbs at Scripps Institute of Oceanography; learns to dive

1947 Hired by U.S. Fish and Wildlife Service to study fish in the Philippine Islands, but gets only as far as Hawaii before being denied FBI clearance; returns to New York to work on her doctorate at NYU and to work at the American Museum of Natural History

1949   Travels to South Pacific to study fish for the U.S. Navy; divorces Umaki

1950   Marries Dr. Ilias Papakonstantinou; receives Ph.D in zoology from NYU; receives Fulbright scholarship to study fish in the Red Sea

1952   Daughter Hera is born

1953   *Lady with a Spear*, her first book, is published

1954   Daughter Aya is born

1955   Becomes founder and executive director of Cape Haze Marine Laboratory in Sarasota, Florida

1956   Son Tak is born

1958   Son Nikolas is born; conducts groundbreaking experiments in shark training

1959   Sets a women's world record for freshwater diving

1966   Divorces Papakonstantinou

1967   Leaves Cape Haze Marine Laboratory

1968   Becomes professor at University of Maryland

1969   *The Lady and the Sharks,* her second book, is published

1972   Studies garden eels near Elat, Israel

1973   Studies "sleeping" sharks in Mexico

1979   Begins conservation efforts in the Red Sea

1981   Takes first ride on whale shark

1986   Makes the first of many submersible dives

1992   Retires officially from the University of Maryland but continues teaching, leading research expeditions and writing scientific and popular articles

1997   Marries Henry Yoshinobu Kon

1999   Teaches last class at University of Maryland but continues to dive and study sandfish and sharks

2000   Leads research expeditions to the South Pacific and La Paz, Mexico; maintains lab spaces at the University of Maryland and the Mote Marine Laboratory (formerly the Cape Haze Marine Laboratory)

2004   Plans six-week research dive in Papua, New Guinea, to celebrate her 82nd birthday

HOW TO BECOME A MARINE BIOLOGIST

THE JOB

Marine biologists study and work with sea creatures in their natural environment, the oceans of the world, and tidal pools along shorelines, as well as in laboratories. These scientists are interested in knowing how the ocean's changing conditions, such as temperature and chemical pollutants, can affect the plants and animals that live there. For example, what happens when certain species become extinct or are no longer safe to be eaten? Marine biologists can begin to understand how the world's food supply is diminished and help come up with solutions that can change such problem situations.

The work of these scientists is also important for improving and controlling sport and commercial fishing. Through underwater exploration, marine biologists have discovered that the world's coral reefs are being damaged by humans. They have also charted the migration of whales and counted the decreasing numbers of certain species. They have observed dolphins being accidentally caught in tuna fishermen's nets. By writing reports and research papers about such discoveries, a marine biologist can inform others about problems that need attention and begin to make important changes that could help the world.

To study plants and animals, marine biologists spend some of their work time in the ocean wearing wetsuits to keep warm (because of the frigid temperature below the surface of the sea) and scuba gear to breathe underwater. They gather specimens with a slurp gun, which sucks fish into a specimen bag without injuring them. They must learn how to conduct their research without damaging the marine environment, which is delicate. Marine biologists must also face the threat to their own safety from dangerous fish and underwater conditions.

Marine biologists also study life in tidal pools along the shoreline. They might collect specimens at the same time of day for days at a time. They would keep samples from different pools separate and keep records of the pool's location and the types and measurements of the specimens taken. These practices ensure that the studies are as accurate as possible. After collecting specimens, marine biologists keep them in a portable aquarium tank on board the ship. After returning to land, which may not be for weeks or months, marine biologists study specimens in a laboratory, often with other scientists working on the same study. They might, for example, check the amount of oxygen in a sea turtle's bloodstream to learn how the turtles can stay underwater for so long, or measure elements in the blood of an arctic fish to discover how it can survive frigid temperatures.

REQUIREMENTS

High School

If you are interested in this career, begin your preparations by taking plenty of high school science classes, such as biology, chemistry, and earth science. Also take math classes and computer-science classes, all of which will give you skills that you will use in doing research. In addition, take English classes, which will also help you develop research skills as well as writing skills. And, because you will probably need to extend your education beyond the level of a bachelor's degree, consider taking a foreign language. Many graduate programs require their students to meet a foreign-language requirement.

Postsecondary Training

In college, take basic science courses such as biology, botany, and chemistry. However, your class choices don't end there. For instance, in biology you might be required to choose from marine invertebrate biology, ecology, oceanography, genetics, animal physiology, plant physiology, and aquatic-plant biology. You might also be required to choose several more specific classes from such choices as ichthyology, vertebrate structure, population biology, developmental biology, biology of microorganisms, evolution, and cell biology. Classes in other subjects will also be required, such as computer science, math (including algebra, trigonometry, calculus, analytical geometry, and statistics), and physics.

Although it is possible to get a job as a marine biologist with just a bachelor's degree, such jobs will likely be low-paying technician positions with little advancement opportunities. Most marine biologists have a master's or doctoral degree. The American Society of Limnology and Oceanography website (http://www.aslo.org) has links to programs offering graduate degrees in aquatic science. Students at the graduate level begin to develop an area of specialization, such as aquatic chemical ecology (the study of chemicals and their effect on aquatic environments) and bioinformatics (the use of computer science, math, and statistics to analyze genetic information). Master's degree programs generally take two to three years to complete. Programs leading to a Ph.D. typically take four to five years to complete.

Certification or Licensing

If you are going to be diving, organizations like the Professional Association of Diving Instructors provide basic certification. Training for scientific diving is more in-depth and requires passing an exam. It is also critical that divers learn cardiopulmonary resuscitation (CPR) and first aid. Also, if you'll be handling hazardous materials such as formaldehyde, strong acids, or radioactive nucleotides, you must be licensed.

Other Requirements

You should have an ability to ask questions and solve problems, observe small details carefully, do research, and analyze mathematical information. You should be inquisitive and must be able to think for yourself. This quality is essential to the scientific method. You must use your creative ability and be inventive in order to design experiments. Working in the field often requires some strength and physical endurance, particularly if you are scuba diving or if you are doing fieldwork in tide pools, which can involve hiking over miles of shore at low tide, keeping your footing on weedy rocks, and lifting and turning stones to find specimens.

EXPLORING

Explore this career and your interest in it by joining your high school's science club. If the club is involved in any type of projects or experiments, you will have the opportunity to begin learning to work with others on a team as well as develop your science and lab skills. If you are lucky enough to live in a city with an aquarium, be sure to get either paid or volunteer work there. This opportunity is an excellent way to learn about marine life and about the life of a marine biologist. Visit Sea Grant's marine careers website (http://www.marinecareers.net) for links to information on internships, volunteerships, and other activities, such as sea camps.

You can begin diving training while you are in high school. If you are between the ages of 10 and 14, you can earn a junior open-water diver certification. When you turn 15, you can upgrade your certification to open-water diver.

EMPLOYERS

Employers in this field range from pharmaceutical companies researching marine sources for medicines to federal agencies that regulate marine fisheries, such as the fisheries division of the National Oceanographic and Atmospheric Administration. Aquariums hire marine biologists to collect and study specimens.

After acquiring many years of experience, marine biologists with Ph.D.'s may be eligible for faculty positions at a school like the Scripps Institute of Oceanography or the University of Washington.

Marine-products companies that manufacture carrageenan and agar (extracted from algae and used as thickening agents in foods) hire marine biologists to design and carry out research.

Jobs in marine biology are based mostly in coastal areas, though some biologists work inland as university professors or perhaps as paleontologists, who search for and study marine fossils.

STARTING OUT

With a bachelor's degree only, you may be able to get a job as a laboratory technician in a state or federal agency. Some aquaria will hire you straight out of college, but generally it's easier to get a paid position if you've worked as a volunteer at an aquarium. You'll need a more advanced degree to get into more technical positions such as consulting, writing for scientific journals, and conducting research.

Websites are good resources for employment information. If you can find the human resources section of an aquarium's home page, it will tell you whom to contact to find out about openings and may even provide job listings. Federal agencies may also have websites with human resource information.

Professors who know you as a student might be able to help you locate a position through their contacts in the professional world.

Another good way to make contacts is by attending conferences or seminars sponsored by aquatic science organizations such as the American Society of Limnology and Oceanography or the Mid-Atlantic Marine Education Association.

ADVANCEMENT

Lab technicians with four-year degrees may advance to become senior lab techs after years with the same lab. Generally, though, taking on greater responsibility or getting into more technical work means having more education. Those wanting to do research (in any setting) will need a graduate degree or at least to be working on one. To get an administrative position with a marine-products company or a faculty position at a university, marine biologists need at least a master's degree, and those wanting to become senior scientists at a marine station or full professors must have a doctoral degree.

EARNINGS

Salaries vary quite a lot depending on factors such as the person's level of education, the type of work (research, teaching, etc.), the size, location, and type of employer (for example, large university, government agency, or private company), and the person's level of work experience. According to the National Association of Colleges and Employers' *Salary Survey* of September 2003, those seeking their first job and holding bachelor's degrees in biological sciences had average salary offers of $29,456. The American Society of Limnology and Oceanography reports that those with bachelor's degrees may start out working for federal government agencies at the pay grades GS-5 to GS-7. In 2004 the yearly earnings at the GS-5 level ranged from $24,075 to $31,302, and yearly earnings at the GS-7 level ranged from $29,821 to $38,767. Income for marine biologists who hold full-time positions at colleges and universities will be similar to those of other full-time faculty. The American Association of University Professors' *Annual Report on the Economic Status of the Profession 2003–2004* found that college teachers (regardless of their subject area) averaged a yearly income of approximately $66,475. It also reports that professors averaged the following salaries by rank: full professors, $88,591; associate professors, $63,063; assistant professors,

$52,788; and instructors, $38,501. Marine biologists who hold top-ranking positions and have much experience, such as senior research scientists, may make more than these amounts.

Benefits vary by employer but often include such extras as health insurance and retirement plans.

WORK ENVIRONMENT

Most marine biologists don't actually spend a lot of time diving. However, researchers might spend a couple of hours periodically breathing from a scuba tank below some waters, like Monterey Bay or the Gulf of Maine. They might gather samples from the deck of a large research vessel during a two-month expedition, or they might meet with several other research biologists.

In most marine biology work, some portion of time is spent in the lab, analyzing samples of seawater or collating data on a computer. Many hours are spent in solitude, reading papers in scientific journals or writing papers for publication.

Instructors or professors work in classrooms interacting with students and directing student lab work.

Those who work for an aquarium, as consultants for private corporations, or in universities work an average of 40 to 50 hours a week.

OUTLOOK

Generally speaking, there are more marine biologists than there are paying positions at present. Changes in the earth's environment, such as global warming and increased levels of heavy metals in the global water cycle, will most likely prompt more research and result in slightly more jobs in different subfields.

Greater need for smart management of the world's fisheries, research by pharmaceutical companies into deriving medicines from marine organisms, and cultivation of marine food alternatives, such as seaweeds and plankton, are other factors that may increase the demand for marine biologists in the near future. Because of strong competition for jobs, however, employment should grow about as fast as the average.

TO LEARN MORE ABOUT MARINE BIOLOGISTS

BOOKS

Byatt, Andrew, Alastair Fothergill, Martha Holmes, and David Attenborough. *Blue Planet.* New York: DK Publishing, 2002.

Doris, Ellen, and Len Rubenstein. *Marine Biology.* Real Kids, Real Science Books. New York: Thames & Hudson, 1994.

Goodson, Gar and Phillip J. Weisgerber. *Fishes of the Pacific Coast: From Alaska to Peru.* Palo Alto, Calif.: Stanford University Press, 1987.

MacQuitty, Miranda. *Eyewitness: Shark.* New York: DK Publishing, 2000.

Waller, Geoffrey, ed. *SeaLife: A Complete Guide to the Marine Environment.* Washington, D.C.: Smithsonian Institution Press, 1996.

ORGANIZATIONS AND WEBSITES

The education and outreach section of American Institute of Biological Sciences' (AIBS) website has information on a number of careers in biology.

American Institute of Biological Sciences
1444 Eye Street, NW, Suite 200
Washington, D.C., 20005
Tel: 202-628-1500
http://www.aibs.org

Visit American Society of Limnology and Oceanography's (ASLO) website for information on careers and education. For information on membership and publications, contact
American Society of Limnology and Oceanography
5400 Bosque Boulevard, Suite 680
Waco, TX 76710
Tel: 800-929-2756
Email: business@aslo.org
http://www.aslo.org

For information on volunteer programs for in-state students and college internships, contact

National Aquarium in Baltimore
Conservation Education Department-Internships
501 East Pratt Street
Baltimore, MD 21202
Tel: 410-576-3800
http://aqua.org

This center for research and education in global science currently runs more than 300 research programs and uses a fleet of four ships to conduct expeditions over the entire globe. For more information, contact

Scripps Institution of Oceanography
University of California–San Diego
8602 La Jolla Shores Drive
La Jolla, CA 92037
http://www-sio.ucsd.edu

HOW TO BECOME A PROFESSIONAL DIVER

THE JOB

Most job opportunities for divers and diving technicians are with commercial diving contractors. The work is frequently dirty, exhausting, and dangerous, and the duties vary greatly. Some common underwater jobs include inspecting structures or equipment using visual, photographic, or videotape methods; operating hand or power tools in mechanical construction or repair; cleaning marine growth from structures; welding or cutting in salvage, repair, or construction functions; and surveying for geological or biological research teams.

Diving technicians do not always work below the water; sometimes they work at the surface, as experts in the life-support system for divers and in the management of the equipment. These technicians work with the controls that supply the proper mixture of gases for the diver to breathe, maintain the correct pressures in the hoses leading to the underwater worker, and act as the communicator and life-support partner of the diver. They also monitor water depth, conditions inside diving bells and chambers, and decompression schedules for divers. This is a highly skilled position involving many responsibilities, and it is vital to the success of all deepwater diving operations.

It is possible in the future that the scientific and technological demands made on the life-support team may cause the development of a group of specialists who do not dive. However, the usual practice now is for divers to work both underwater and on deck.

Other important areas of employment for divers and diving technicians are in oceanographic research and underwater military engineering. While the total number of technicians engaged in these activities is relatively small, it may increase as it becomes more desirable to extract minerals from the ocean floor. Even during peacetime, military diving crews are needed in rescue and reclamation.

Divers and diving technicians also work as recreation specialists. They may be employed by dive resorts, dive charter boats, municipal recreation departments, dive stores, or postsecondary institutions. The work performed will vary depending on the employer's specific business, but it frequently includes teaching the general public about recreational diving, supervising and coordinating recreational dives at resorts and on cruise ships, teaching diving lessons and selling equipment at a retail dive store, and repairing equipment for customers of a dive store.

Newly hired technicians are normally assigned to organize the shop and care for and maintain all types of company equipment. Soon, they will be assigned a similar job on a diving boat or platform. When on a diving operation, technicians help maintain a safe and efficient operation by providing topside or surface support for the divers: They assist them with equipment, supply hoses, communications, necessary tools, and lines. As a diver's tender, technicians may monitor and control diving descent and ascent rates, breathing gas supplies, and decompression schedules. They must also be able to assist in an emergency and help treat a diver injured in an accident or suffering from the bends.

As technicians gain experience in company procedures and jobs, they are given more responsibility. Technicians usually can start underwater work within a few months to two years after being hired, depending on the technician's skills and the company's needs.

Technicians' first dives are shallow and relatively easy; subsequent dives match their ability and competence. With time and experience, they may advance to work deep-dive bell and saturation diving systems. Saturation divers are gradually compressed in an on-deck chamber, as they would be when diving, and then transferred to and from the work site inside a pressurized bell. These divers stay in a pressure-controlled environment for extended periods.

All of the personnel on a diving crew should know how to care for and use a wide variety of equipment. Some of the commonly used diving equipment includes air compressors, decompression chambers, high-pressure breathing-gas storage tanks, pressure regulators and gas regulating systems, hoses and fittings for handling air and gas, and communications equipment.

A diver's personal equipment ranges from simple scuba, now seldom used, to full face masks; lightweight and heavy helmets for both air and helium/oxygen use; diving bells; and diving suits, from wet suits to the heavy dry suits that can be bolted to a breastplate to which the heavy helmet is attached. For cold water and deep or long-duration dives, a hot-water suit may be used. This allows a flow of warm water supplied from the surface to be passed through a loose-fitting wet suit on the diver's body, protecting the diver from loss of body heat.

Commercial diving crews use simple hand tools, including hammers, crescent wrenches, screwdrivers, and pliers. Items such as wire cutters and volt/ohm meters are often needed. Divers should be versatile and may also be expected to use many types of power tools, as well as sophisticated and often delicate instruments, such as video and camera equipment, measuring instruments, ultrasonic probes, and metal detection devices. Knowledge of arc welding equipment and underwater arc or other metal-cutting equipment is very important for many kinds of work, such as salvage, construction, or repair and modification of underwater structures. These needs are often associated with underwater petroleum explorations, well-drilling, or management of piping systems.

REQUIREMENTS
High School
Typical basic requirements for enrollment in a diving program are a high school diploma or its equivalent, reading comprehension, completion of three to four years of language and communications subjects, at least one year of algebra, and one year of physics or chemistry with laboratory work.

Postsecondary Training

The best way to train for this career is to attend one of the postsecondary schools and colleges that offer an organized program, usually two years in length, to prepare such technicians. Diving technicians are specialized engineering technicians. Therefore, they need a basic theoretical and practical background in science. Mastery of several construction-type work skills is also necessary. A typical postsecondary program in marine diving technology is designed to develop the skills and knowledge required of a commercial diver, an understanding of the marine environment, and an ability to communicate well.

The first year's study includes such courses as seamanship and small-boat handling, basic diving, drafting, basic welding, technical writing, advanced diving, fundamentals of marine engines and compressors, marine welding, physical oceanography, and marine biology. Often, students participate in a summer cooperative work-study program of supervised ocean dives before the second year of courses begins.

Second-year courses typically include underwater construction, biological oceanography, physics, fundamentals of electronics, machine shop operations, underwater operations, advanced diving systems, basic emergency medical technology, and speech and communications. The second year also may include fundamentals of photography or a special project that relates specifically to diving or life-support technology. Additional studies such as economics or other general studies must usually be taken.

Programs for prospective recreation specialists also focus on understanding the marine environment and developing communications skills, but instead of welding, drafting, and other technical classes, these programs require the development of basic business skills. Courses in small business management, introduction to marketing, organizational behavior, computer science, and business law are usually offered. Schools that provide these programs often have special admission requirements relating to swimming ability and skills.

When you seek employment, you usually find that many employers require completion of a recognized training program or documentation of comparable experience. Additionally, an emergency medical technician certificate is valuable and may be required by some companies.

Certification or Licensing

There are no special requirements for licenses at the entry level in the United States. However, the United Kingdom and some of the North Sea countries do have specific requirements for divers, which can be met only by training in their countries.

Certification is required for recreational diving instructors and is available through such organizations as Professional Association of Diving Instructors, National Association of Underwater Instructors, and the YMCA. Certification for commercial divers is not required, but is available through the Association of Commercial Divers International.

For specific work beyond entry level, a welding certificate may be required. Also, a certification in nondestructive testing (NDT) may enhance your opportunities. Both of these certificates are specific and beyond entry level. Employers will be able to specify the method of obtaining the special certificates they desire.

Other Requirements

Employment in areas other than commercial diving may impose more specific requirements. A specialty in photography, electronics, oceanography, biology, marine culture, or construction engineering may open other doors of opportunity for the diving technician.

You need more than excellent diving skills; diving is just the way they reach their work site. You should be mechanically inclined and able to operate and maintain a wide variety of equipment. You must understand drawings and simple blueprints; be familiar with piping and valves; know how to handle high-pressure gases, bottles, and gauges; and be able to write accurate reports, keep records, and do paperwork. An understanding of the physical and biological elements of the marine environment and the ability to work as a member of a team are crucial.

Recreation specialists need excellent communications skills. With some employers, business management, marketing, and computer skills are also important.

Physical requirements for the career include overall good health, at least normal physical strength, sound respiratory functions, normal or better eyesight, and good hand-eye coordination and manual dexterity.

EXPLORING

You can find information about training schools in trade journals and sports publications. Libraries are a good place to look for program listings and descriptions. It is a good idea to contact several training programs and compare the offerings to your own individual needs. Make sure to ask about employment prospects for future graduates of each program.

A visit to one or more potential employers would certainly be of benefit. While observation of an offshore job would be difficult, a tour of the company shop, a look at its equipment, and a chance to talk to technicians should be informative and worthwhile.

Become proficient in scuba diving and outdoor swimming and diving. The experience of learning to feel at home in water and underwater not only can help you pass entry tests for a formal preparatory program but also can allow you to find out if you really are suited for the career.

EMPLOYERS

The major employers of diving technicians are companies that search for petroleum and natural gas from undersea oil fields. Hydroelectric power generating plants, dams, heavy industry, and sanitation plants that have cooling water lines or water discharges are also a source of work for divers and surface crews. Certain ship repairs, usually of an emergency nature, require divers who can repair the trouble at sea or in dock, without placing the ship in dry dock to correct the problem.

While some work is being done in aquaculture, marine culture, and ocean mining, these areas are currently relatively undeveloped. While the potential for these fields is great and the possibilities for divers exciting, the total employment in these areas is presently small.

STARTING OUT

Commercial diving contractors, where the majority of diving technicians seek employment, have in the past recruited personnel from U.S. Navy training programs, informal apprenticeship programs, and through personal contacts. These employees had to learn on the job.

As diving technology advanced and diving equipment and techniques became more sophisticated, contractors looked more and more to schools to provide qualified entry-level help. Today, most commercial diving contractors primarily rely on approved schools to meet their entry-level personnel needs. Some contractors will hire only graduates of diving training programs.

Schools with diving technician programs usually have three or more staff members with professional commercial diving experience. These instructors keep abreast of the diving industry through occasional summer work, consultation, and professional and personal contacts. These contacts enable them to assess industry needs and to offer job placement help.

Major offshore contractors and other potential employers may visit schools with diving programs each year before graduation to interview prospective employees. Some employers offer summer work to students who have completed one year of a two-year program.

Some employers contact schools whenever they need additional diving personnel. The school staff then directs them to interested job seekers. While many graduates find jobs in oil-drilling operations or other large industries, a few graduates find positions as diving school instructors, marine culture technicians, photographers/writers, marine research technicians, and submersible pilots.

You can also enter a diving career by joining the U.S. Navy or specialized units of the Marines, Army Corps of Engineers, or Merchant Marine Corps. Some U.S. military operations for salvage, recovery of sunken ships, or rescue require deepwater divers and life-support skills. Usually Navy and other experienced diving personnel can obtain civilian employment, but they often need to learn a wider range of skills for underwater construction or other work.

ADVANCEMENT

A well-trained, highly motivated diver or diving technician can expect to advance steadily, depending on personal competence and the employer's needs. Over a three- to five-year period a technician may be a shop hand, a tender (tending equipment and maintaining gear), a combination diver/tender, a diver, lead diver, and possibly supervisor of a diving crew. Or a technician may advance from surface support duties to supervisor of surface support or supervisor of a diving crew, possibly within three to five years. The nondiving life-support career, however, is much more limited in terms of employment opportunities than the combined diving and support career. Management opportunities within the company are also a possibility for qualified divers. Those who want greater opportunities for earnings, independence, and growth may start their own business as a contractor or consultant.

EARNINGS

Earnings in this career vary widely and depend on factors such as location, nature of the job, and the technician's skills or experience. A technician working in commercial diving might work almost anyplace in the oceans, rivers, and lakes of the world, although in the United States there is much work to be found in the Gulf of Mexico and in the Louisiana coastline, areas close to offshore wells. Some types of work, primarily union jobs, pay the employee on an hourly or daily basis.

Recent graduates of diving technician programs often start in nondiving positions as tenders and earn around $10 to $11 an hour. An entry-level diver spends 200 days offshore and earns $100 take home pay per day on average, or between $20,000 and $24,000 a year. After several years of experience, a diver can earn $40,000 to $70,000 a year. The prevailing non-union wage is about $33 to $41 an hour. The most experienced divers, who have at least 10 years experience can earn $60,000 to $100,000 a year.

Some contract jobs call for time on and time off, such as a 30 days on/30 days off rotation, and the pay will reflect at least a certain amount of the off-time as full-time pay. An example of a rotational job would be service work on an exploratory oil-drilling vessel where diving crew members live aboard for their on-shift period and perform any work required during that time. Wages earned under an organized union contract are typically higher, but the employee receives pay only for days worked. Because divers typically earn well, many divers choose to work only during the diving season, which takes place from June to December.

Employees of diving contractors typically receive life and health insurance benefits. Some companies also provide paid vacation time.

WORK ENVIRONMENT

Commercial divers must possess numerous technical job skills. Working conditions may vary tremendously depending upon the nature of the work, the duration of the job, and the geographic location. Recreation specialists are frequently responsible for the welfare of inexperienced divers. Although they may work in a resort, under seemingly idyllic conditions, satisfying the needs of a group of diverse individuals may sometimes be stressful.

Some offshore sites include boats ranging from under 100 feet long to much longer oceangoing ships. Also, oil drilling vessels and many types of barges provide working and living bases for diving technicians.

Working hours or shifts offshore may only require the diving crew to be available if needed, as is common on drilling vessels. More often, however, as in construction work or jobs that are continuous and predictable in nature, the dive crew will work up to 12 hours a day, seven days a week. As might be expected, the more rigorous work provides greater pay.

Living conditions aboard a ship or barge are usually comfortable. Rooms may accommodate from two to as many as eight people, depending on vessel size. Food, of course, is furnished on all rigs where crews must live aboard.

Diving technicians are taught to be conscious of appropriate clothing and safety practices and to follow these guidelines as they work in the potentially dangerous conditions encountered in deepwater diving.

Offshore work, especially construction diving, is rigorous and often physically demanding. Persons entering this field must be physically fit. Companies commonly place a maximum age limit, usually 30 to 32 years, for entry-level employees seeking to become divers. Although many divers work well into their 40s or 50s or older, long-duration deep diving is considered a young person's work.

Travel, excitement, and some amount of risk are a part of the diving technician's life. While on the job, technicians should be self-starters, showing initiative and the ability to work independently as well as on a team.

People who choose a career in diving should be ready to adapt to a lifestyle that seldom offers stable home and family life. They must be able to follow the work and can expect occasional changes in job locations. There is also the reality of an uncertain work schedule, where a job might last for months or where the only available work may be on a short-term basis. Offshore work tends to run in a "feast or famine" pattern.

Divers and diving technicians must be confident of their own ability to cope with the uncertainties and risks of deepwater diving. They must be able to analyze and solve problems without panic or confusion. For most divers, there is real satisfaction in confidently and successfully performing tasks in an unconventional setting.

OUTLOOK

The world is increasingly turning to the sea to supply mineral resources, new and additional sources of food and medicine, transportation, and national defense. This growth in marine activity has resulted in a continuing demand for qualified diving technicians. According to diving schools, there are approximately two to three jobs for every qualified graduate of technical diving programs. New graduates, however, must make a long-term commitment to become successful divers. Entry-level positions can be low-paying and mostly on dry land, but with a few years of experience, gradually spending more time in the water and learning skills on the job, they usually are rewarded both in terms of pay and job satisfaction.

In the past few decades, the greatest demand for skilled diving technicians has been related to the search for more petroleum and natural gas from undersea oil fields. With the production of oil and gas from the oceans, there was a virtual explosion in the amount of work and the numbers of people employed. Whether this activity will be a source of new jobs in the future is uncertain. Employment will depend on levels of drilling activity, which, in turn, will depend on world oil prices. Traditionally, divers have been able to find jobs even during tough economic times, although it will take longer before a newcomer gets "wet" on an assignment. Diving technicians also have the flexibility to switch into the commercial diving areas in order to take advantage of job openings.

TO LEARN MORE ABOUT PROFESSIONAL DIVERS

BOOKS

Barsky, Steven M. *The Simple Guide to Snorkeling Fun.* Flagstaff, Ariz.: Best Publishing, 1999.

Graver, Dennis K. *Scuba Diving: Official Instruction Manual of the YMCA of the USA.* 3rd ed. Champaign, Ill.: Human Kinetics, 2003.

Jackson, Jack. *Diving: The World's Best Sites.* New York: Rizzoli, 1997.

Joiner, James T. *NOAA Diving Manual: Diving for Science and Technology.* Flagstaff, Ariz.: Best Publishing, 2001.

Rossier, Robert N. *Diving Like a Pro: 101 Ways to Improve Your Scuba Skills and Safety.* Flagstaff, Ariz.: Best Publishing, 1999.

ORGANIZATIONS AND WEBSITES

For information on diving instruction and certification, contact Professional Association of Diving Instructors (PADI).

Professional Association of Diving Instructors

30151 Tomas Street

Rancho Santa Margarita, CA 92688-2125

Tel: 800-729-7234

http://www.padi.com

To learn more about the latest news in scuba diving, visit *Scuba Diving Magazine's* website.

Scuba Diving Magazine

http://www.scubadiving.com

TO LEARN MORE ABOUT EUGENIE CLARK AND OCEAN LIFE

BOOKS

Brooks, Felicity. *Seas and Oceans*. Tulsa: EDC Publishing, 1999.

Butts, Ellen, and Joyce Schwartz. *Eugenie Clark: Adventures of a Shark Scientist*. North Haven, Conn.: Linnet Books, 2000.

Castro, Peter, and Michael Huber. *Marine Biology*. 4th ed. Boston: McGraw Hill, 2003.

Clark, Eugenie. *Lady with a Spear*. New York: Harper and Row, 1953.

———. *The Lady and the Sharks*. New York: Harper and Row, 1969.

Clark, Eugenie, and Ann McGovern. *The Desert Beneath the Sea*. New York: Scholastic Inc., 1991.

Collard, Sneed. *The Deep-Sea Floor*. Watertown, Mass.: Charlesbridge, 2003.

Dipper, Frances and Trevor Day. *Guide to the Oceans*. London: DK Publishing, 2002.

Dunn, Margery, ed. *Exploring Your World: The Adventure of Geography*. Washington, D.C.: The National Geographic Society, 1993.

Earle, Sylvia A. *Dive: My Adventures in the Deep Frontier*. Washington, D.C.: The National Geographic Society, 1999.

Johnson, Jinny. *Children's Guide to Sea Creatures*. New York: Simon & Schuster Books for Young Readers, 1998.

Layman, Dale. *Biology Demystified*. New York: McGraw-Hill, 2003.

MacQuitty, Miranda. *Ocean*. London: DK Publishing, 2000.

———. *Shark*. London: DK Publishing, 2000.

McGovern, Ann. *Adventures of the Shark Lady: Eugenie Clark Around the World*. New York: Scholastic Inc., 1999.

McKenzie, Michelle. *The Insiders' Guide to the Monterey Bay Aquarium*. Monterey, Calif.: Monterey Bay Aquarium Foundation, 2004.

Parker, Steve. *Fish*. London: DK Publishing, 2000.

Passport to the Islands. Long Beach, Calif.: Aquarium of the Pacific, 2004.

Ross, Michael Elsohn. *Fish Watching with Eugenie Clark.* Minneapolis: Carolrhoda Books, Inc., 2000.

Taylor, Ron, and Valerie Taylor. *Sharks: Silent Hunters of the Deep*. Sydney: Reader's Digest, 2001.

The World Almanac and Book of Facts 2002. New York: World Almanac Books, 2002.

Vogel, Carole G. *The Restless Sea: Ocean Wildlife*. New York: Franklin Watts, 2003.

ARTICLES

Clark, Eugenie. "Down the Cayman Wall." *National Geographic*, November 1988, 712–730.

———. "Flashlight Fish of the Red Sea." *National Geographic*, November 1978, 719–728.

———. "Hidden Life of an Undersea Desert." *National Geographic*, July 1983, 129–144.

———. "Into the Lairs of 'Sleeping' Sharks." *National Geographic*, April 1975, 570–584.

———. "Sharks: Magnificent and Misunderstood." *National Geographic*, August 1981, 138–186.

———. "Sharks at 2,000 Feet." *National Geographic*, November 1986, 681–691.

———. "The Red Sea's Gardens of Eels." *National Geographic*, November 1972, 724–734.

——. "The Red Sea's Sharkproof Fish." *National Geographic*, November 1974, 719–727.

——. "The Strangest Sea." *National Geographic*, September 1975, 338–343.

——. "Whale Sharks: Gentle Monsters of the Deep." *National Geographic*, December 1992, 123–138.

Sipchen, Bob. "Do-It-Yourself *Ahoogah*." *The Los Angeles Times,* 6 April 2004, Outdoors section, p. 4.

Stone, Gregory. "Phoenix Islands: A Coral Reef Wilderness Revealed." *National Geographic*, February 2004, 18–65.

Westmorland, Stuart, and Michele Westmorland. "Dive: Papua New Guinea." *Scuba Diving*, January 2004, 59–63.

ORGANIZATIONS AND WEBSITES

The U.S. government's official National Oceanic and Atmospheric Administration (NOAA) website.
http://www.noaa.gov/

A great site featuring pictures of ocean animals. Just click on the animal you are looking for. This is a great site for helping with your homework.
http://mbgnet.mobot.org/salt/animals/

This site contains information on just about any species of fish.
http://www.fishbase.org/search.cfm

Read all about the submersible craft *Alvin*.
http://www.ocean.udel.edu/deepsea/

Visit this site for facts about sharks and problems they face due to overfishing.
http://www.sharktrust.org/index.html

This site contains information on the Nature Conservancy's Rescue the Reef program.
http://www.nature.org

Seacology works to preserve the environments and cultures of islands throughout the globe.
http://www.seacology.org

This is the website of the federated State of Micronesia, a popular spot for deep-sea exploration.
http://www.visit-fsm.org/

This is the website of the International Marinelife Alliance.
http://marine.org

INDEX

Page numbers in *italics* indicate illustrations.

ABOUT THE AUTHOR

Ronald A. Reis is the author of 10 books and numerous articles on subjects ranging from technology to careers. He is the author of *Becoming an Electronic Technician: Securing Your High-Tech Future, Careers in Art and Graphic Design*, and *The Everything Hot Careers Book*. In addition to textbooks on electronics and computer technology, Mr. Reis is the technology department chair at Los Angeles Valley College. He lives with his wife, Karen, in Calabasas, California. They have two daughters and two grandchildren.

DATE DUE

DEMCO 128-5046